Henry Martyn Grout

**The Gospel Invitation Sermons**

Henry Martyn Grout

**The Gospel Invitation Sermons**

ISBN/EAN: 9783743360761

Manufactured in Europe, USA, Canada, Australia, Japa

Cover: Foto ©Lupo / pixelio.de

Manufactured and distributed by brebook publishing software (www.brebook.com)

Henry Martyn Grout

**The Gospel Invitation Sermons**

# The Gospel Invitation:

SERMONS RELATED TO

## THE BOSTON REVIVAL OF 1877.

BOSTON:
LOCKWOOD, BROOKS, AND COMPANY.
1877.

COPYRIGHT
BY
LOCKWOOD, BROOKS & CO.
1877.

*Printed by Rockwell & Churchill.*

# PREFACE.

THIS volume is an outgrowth of the revival now in progress in this city and surrounding region, and still a rising tide. It has been the desire and endeavor of the editor to make it an exponent of the pervading spirit of that work, and of the great moving truths by which it has been promoted. With this intent, eminent pastors of different denominations in the city were invited to contribute to its pages sermons preached in the regular ministrations of the pulpit during this most interesting time, and aimed at the consciences and hearts of men, to bring them to Christ. Contributions of a similar character were solicited from several others, particularly from well-known and widely-honored professors in the different universities and theological institutions of the city and vicinity. It was believed that, not only as expositions of truth, but as showing how the gospel is preached in these centres of intellectual life, these would greatly add to the present interest and permanent value of the book.

It should be said that none of these discourses were at first prepared with any thought of their appearance on the printed page. Nor have they been selected as specimens of fine writing, or well-rounded discussions. They are not offered to the public as exhibitions of either the intellectual power or the rhetorical skill of their authors. But, as earnest and vigorous presentations of truths which God now as at other times is pleased to own for the conversion of men to himself, and as illustrating the extent to which the present revival spirit pervades pulpits of all ecclesiastical names and relations, we anticipate for them a wide and warm welcome. Much has been said of "Boston preaching" and "Boston theology." These phrases would indicate that hereabouts the old faith has given place to a new, and that the sublime truths held and preached by the fathers have been supplanted by another gospel. The following pages can hardly fail to do something to correct such an impression if it anywhere exists.

It will interest the reader to know that Dr. Peabody's is one of his ordinary Sabbath morning discourses to the students of Harvard College; that that by Dean Gray was addressed to his usual congregation, largely composed of young men from the same institution, and of students of the Episcopal Theological School; that Professor Caldwell's is contributed from an ample store of effective revival discourses; and that President Warren's was first preached at a Massachusetts camp-meeting. Both the Sermon and the Monday Lecture, by Rev. Joseph Cook, are printed from stenographer's reports, revised by himself, — the former, preached at the Tabernacle, being hardly more than an excellent outline; while the latter, one of the most powerful and valuable of his winter's course, has been considerably enlarged for its present use.

We congratulate ourselves and our readers on the addition, to all the other good things to be found in these pages, of an occasional and memorable discourse by Professor Park. As revised by himself for this volume it cannot fail to attract and richly repay many readers.

H. M. GROUT.

APRIL, 1877.

# CONTENTS.

### I.
THE CHRISTIAN BELIEVER'S BURDEN, — Page 9
By EDMUND K. ALDEN, D. D., Boston.

### II.
THE OLD FAITH AND THE NEW, — 29
By GEORGE C. LORIMER, D. D., Pastor of Union Temple Baptist Church, Boston.

### III.
LEARN OF ME, — 59
By GEORGE ZABRISKIE GRAY, D. D., Dean of the Episcopal Theological School of Massachusetts, Cambridge.

### IV.
THE SEPARATION OF THE SOUL FROM GOD, — 71
By W. F. MALLALIEU, D. D., Pastor of Second Methodist Episcopal Church, Boston.

### V.
THE DECAY OF WILL, — 88
By REV. S. E. HERRICK, Pastor of Mount Vernon Congregational Church, Boston.

### VI.
COMING TO ONE'S SELF, — 101
By ANDREW P. PEABODY, D. D., Plummer Professor, and Preacher, at Harvard University, Cambridge.

### VII.
THE CRY FOR A CLEANSED HEART, — 114
By REV. ALBERT E. DUNNING, Pastor of Highland Congregational Church, Boston.

### VIII.
GOD'S CONTROVERSY WITH HIS PEOPLE, — 126
By ALEXANDER H. VINTON, D. D., Rector of Emanuel Church, Boston.

## IX.
**God a Consuming Fire,**     139

By Rev. A. J. Gordon, Pastor of Clarendon Street Baptist Church, Boston.

## X.
**God Dismissed,**     153

By Samuel L. Caldwell, D. D., Professor in Newton Theological Institution, Newton Centre.

## XI.
**Jesus of Nazareth Passeth By,**     166

By Rev. Alexander McKenzie, Pastor of the First Church, Cambridge.

## XII.
**Nothing to Do with Christ,**     179

By Rev. William Wilberforce Newton, Rector of St. Paul's Church, Boston.

## XIII.
**The Door Opened and Christ Within,**     197

By Rev. Henry M. Grout, Pastor of Congregational Church, Concord.

## XIV.
**Faith the Source of Faithfulness,**     210

By Rev. Joseph Cook, Boston.

## XV.
**Our Two Harvests,**     229

By Rufus Ellis, D. D., Minister of the First Church of Christ, Boston.

## XVI.
**The Gospel Invitation,**     238

By W. F. Warren, D. D., President of Boston University.

## XVII.
**The Permanence of Moral Character,**     263

By Rev. Joseph Cook, Boston.

## XVIII.
**The Prominence of the Atonement,**     299

By Edwards A. Park, D. D., Professor in Andover Theological Seminary, Andover.

# THE GOSPEL INVITATION.

---

*SERMONS.*

# THE CHRISTIAN BELIEVER'S BURDEN.

### BY EDMUND K. ALDEN, D. D.

"I say the truth in Christ, I lie not, my conscience also bearing me witness in the Holy Ghost, that I have great heaviness and continual sorrow in my heart. For I could wish that myself were accursed from Christ, for my brethren, my kinsmen according to the flesh."—*Romans* ix. 1-3.

THE self-sacrificing spirit of Christian love can employ no expression which is extravagant in trying to give utterance to the longings felt for the salvation of others. It exclaims, My soul is in heaviness; I am oppressed with anguish; let anything dreadful happen to myself; let me die a hundred deaths; let me know even the midnight darkness of a castaway — "accursed from Christ," if such a thing could be, might I but deliver you from your impending doom. The very impossibility of the supposition is what gives it its rhetorical power.

Paul had just exclaimed, "I am persuaded that neither death, nor life, nor angels, nor principalities, nor powers, nor things present, nor things to come, nor height, nor depth, nor any other creature, shall be able to separate us from the love of God, which is in Christ Jesus our Lord." Rejoicing in this living inner fellowship of the Father and of the Son, it is with all calmness and sobriety that he adds, "I say the truth in Christ;" it is the love of Christ in my soul which leads me thus to express myself. "I lie not, my conscience also bearing me witness in the Holy Ghost." I know whereof I affirm, — it is that Spirit who "maketh intercession for us with groanings which cannot be uttered," who beareth me witness. "I have great heaviness and continual sorrow in my heart" in your behalf.

It must be borne in mind that the Christian experience of a joy which is "unspeakable," and the Christian experience of a sorrow whose inward groanings "cannot be uttered," are both from the same source, the fruit of the same Spirit; so that if one is known, both may be known, though not always in the same degree, nor always consciously at the same hour.

In speaking, therefore, of the burden which sometimes weighs heavily upon Christian hearts, let it not be supposed that the blessedness of the Christian's hope is thereby excluded, for the burden and the blessedness go together. But there are times when the burden is especially prominent. Such a time we are now passing through.

As our Lord's mental anguish in behalf of guilty men is termed "the travail of his soul," so a similar anguish felt by his people is represented by the same word. Thus Paul addresses the Galatians: "My little children, for whom I travail in birth again, until Christ be formed in you." The Apostle knew in some measure what it was to participate in that painful distress which the Lord Jesus felt in his agonizing desires for the salvation of men. The reason was that the Spirit of Christ in some measure dwelt within him,— the Holy Spirit, who is continuing and completing the work of Christ on earth, through the instrumentality of Christian believers in whom he abides and through whom he works.

This burden of anxiety which sometimes presses heavily upon Christian hearts, in behalf of their fellow-men who are still in sin, is "because the love of God is shed abroad in our hearts by the Holy Ghost which is given unto us,"—that love of the Father which gave his only-begotten Son that he might die for man; that love of the Son which led him to surrender himself to an ignominious and sacrificial death; and that love of the Spirit which pleads and strives with men; which is grieved by their unbelief, and which in many ways cries, "To-day, after so long a time, if ye will hear his voice, harden not your hearts." How little does any affectionate Christian heart, weighed down with whatever burden of anxiety for others, know of the intensity and depth of that yearning, divine love which, taking no pleasure in the death of the sinner, with long-suffering patience, waiting to be gracious, continues to plead, "Turn ye, turn ye; why will ye die?"

As it is an evidence that the Spirit of God is within the soul, when the soul feels a pressure of tender anxiety for perishing men, for the same reason the soul is sustained under the pressure. The Holy Spirit operates in accordance with the laws of the mental constitution, and does no violence to the human mind. One of his significant names is "the Spirit of Truth;" and one of his offices is to enlighten the mind in the knowledge of the truth. When, therefore, he is manifesting his presence through an unusual anxiety experienced by a Christian heart in behalf of men who are still in sin, we may be sure there is reason for this anxiety. It is produced by a clear discernment of truths — truths, when believed, of most impressive significance.

One of these truths is *the intrinsic worth associated with the imminent danger of our fellow-men.* Sometimes we look upon people in the mass, a crowd of human beings jostling against each other for a little while along life's thoroughfare, and then passing away. But now our eyes are opened, and in every man we look upon we see an immortal spirit, gifted with the capacities and opportunities, subject also to the exposures, of such a spirit. A violator of the law of God, he is amenable to the just penalty of that law. Continuing an unbeliever in Christ, he abides under condemnation. As swiftly as the precious days, weeks, and years are flying by, so swiftly are they bearing him on to death and the judgment after death. He is thoughtlessly wasting his only probation. Whatever else he may be, remaining away from Christ, he is unprepared both to live and to die. So living he is adding sin to sin, treasuring up "wrath against the day of wrath." So dying, the day of grace has ended, and his soul must forever perish.

Surrender to the seriousness of this thought. Apply it to some one individual. Consider what it means for this man to lose his soul; hold your mind to the consideration and bear upon your heart his heavy woe. Think of another and of another. Can you add the thought that some of them are your own friends, for whose safety you would be ready to sacrifice your life? Can you add the thought that entire families are thus exposed? That there are several hundred in a Christian congregation who are thus exposed? That you live in a world of beings in the same peril? That you are mingling with them all the time in society and in business? That some of them you are influencing every day by example and conversation?

Let any one carry upon a sympathizing, affectionate heart such a weight as this, and will there not be some experience of heavy sorrow? Do you say, "I cannot bear it, and I will dismiss the thought?" But you have not thus lifted the woe which rests upon your fellow-men. The fact still abides true that they are going down to death. To disregard the fact is to give them up to perish without an effort for their salvation. That surely is not the spirit of him who came to seek and to save the lost. If, therefore, the heart of Christ is in us, we shall not only feel the burden of human woe, we shall long intensely to relieve it.

Accordingly, a second thought is impressed upon the Christian heart by the Holy Spirit,— *the desirableness that these our fellow-men should be saved, associated with the fact that abundant provision is made for their salvation.* We picture the other side in the possible history of a soul; what that soul may become, redeemed from the guilt and pollution of sin, freed from the condemnation of the unbeliever, filled with the blessedness of abiding fellowship with God, living a life consecrated to the service of Christ, triumphing over death, and entering into a glorious immortality — the overhanging woe exchanged forever for superabounding grace. We think of one soul thus saved; of another, and another; of scores, of hundreds; of families, of congregations, of the vast multitudes around us, whose condition weighs upon us with anxiety. The immediate question now becomes, What can I do to save them? Here are abundant provisions for salvation in the revelation of the Gospel of Christ. Here is the promise, "Whosoever shall call upon the name of the Lord shall be saved." Here is the invitation, "Whosoever will, let him take the water of life freely." And now the pressure of anxiety takes this direction: What can I do to lead these souls to believe in Christ? How can I carry this good news to others? How can I proclaim it to all my fellow-men? Upon whom can I impress it as a reality? Whom can I bring to this fountain of everlasting life?

A third consideration begins now to weigh heavily upon the Christian heart, — *the consciousness of personal responsibility to the utmost of the ability and the opportunity afforded us for the salvation of all the souls we can possibly reach, especially for those particularly committed to our care by the providence of God.* We perceive not only that there is provision for their salvation, but that we are appointed by the divine grace imparted unto us to be the instruments of communicating that salvation. We perceive that the Gospel has been given to dwellers in a Christian land for the very purpose of extending it through the world, and that there is no reason why any generation of Christian men should not in their own day diffuse the word of life among all the men of that generation living on the earth, except that they refuse to recognize and to act upon that responsibility. That pressure of responsibility has never been lifted from any generation since Christ left his parting command, "Go ye into all the world and preach the gospel to every creature." It never will be lifted until this world is converted to Christ; and, as the Holy Spirit is more fully received into our waiting souls, we shall feel this pressure more and more. Possibly this is the generation which is to be bowed down under that weight, and which in its conscious weakness is to be made strong by divine strength to bear it, to the conquest of the world to Christ. Certainly whatever people shall receive an apostolic outpouring of the Holy Spirit, will receive as its accompanying fruit an apostolic missionary zeal.

But if the simple possession of the written word puts upon us the responsibility of proclaiming it throughout the world, much more does the possession of divine grace in our own souls bring with it the responsibility of communicating the same to the utmost of our ability to all whom we can reach, especially to those nearest to us, by ties of kindred and affection. We sometimes try to relieve ourselves from this pressure, but not when our souls are filled with the Spirit of God; for it is the Spirit of God who awakens and increases the affectionate anxiety which produces the pressure. There is a serious sense in which we are accountable not only for our own souls, but for scores of other souls; and if they perish through our faithlessness or neglect, their blood will be required at our hand. No parent, no teacher, no pastor, no individual who exerts influence upon others, can escape this responsibility. We shall be called to meet it at the final day. When the Spirit of God takes this truth and holds us to it, it puts upon every one of us a heavy burden.

Bowing down beneath this pressure, the people of God are led to associate with it another, without which they would be utterly overwhelmed, namely, *a sense of entire dependence upon the divine strength both to sustain and to guide, with the assured expectation that the needed strength and guidance will be imparted.* The burdens of anxiety and of responsibility thus pass into a burden of prayer, continuous and importunate prayer, prayer so laden with a weight of promises, that the greater the pressure they produce, the greater their ability to sustain. The same pressure will constrain to the exercise of all possible efforts for the salvation of those for whom we are anxious; and the Holy Spirit, thus yielded to by the submissive soul, will lead on to more fervent prayers and increased efforts, prayer and efforts which will be successful. For, be it remembered, these heavy anxieties resting upon Christian hearts, by which they share with their Lord in "the travail of his soul," fit them also to share at length in the "shall be satisfied," when those souls are born into the kingdom of Christ and become trophies of redemptive grace.

Indeed, it is a special divine appointment that this

should be the method by which the Holy Spirit shall display his presence and power in the renewal of men. When the people of God are in heaviness of heart, borne down under the burden of their anxiety for perishing souls,—a burden which is relieved only by prayer and diligent effort for their salvation, then is the hour of Zion's deliverance; then the Spirit of God interposes, and these souls wrestled and labored for are saved. Thus has it been in the past history of the Church, and thus will it continue. Those who are to be the instruments of communicating the Spirit of God to their fellow-men, must yield themselves to the influences of that Spirit, or his regenerating power will not be mightily exercised in the community where they dwell. If many souls are to be gathered into the kingdom of God, it must be through the importunate pleadings of those in whom the Spirit maketh intercession with groanings which cannot be uttered.

One of the reasons why God has appointed this method of bestowing, is in order that the people of God may prize the blessing when they receive it. The principle that we value what we have wrestled for, applies to God's greatest gift. When, therefore, we begin to pray for the mighty outpouring of the Spirit of God in a community, if our prayer is answered, one of the first results to be expected will be "great heaviness and continual sorrow," pressing upon the Lord's people as a burden of anxiety in behalf of friends and neighbors who are still in sin. The members of a church will take upon their hearts, in a new and unusual manner, the congregation committed to their care. They will carry the burden day after day, and week after week. It will constrain them to persevering and importunate prayer. It will impart a new tenderness of affection to all their efforts for the salvation of those whom they can in any way approach. It will lead them to put away all hindrances to the immediate and powerful operations of the Spirit of God. It will unite together as never before, in a common anxiety and common labors. It will induce them to surrender everything else in the earnest and continuous endeavor to call men into the fellowship of Christ. To this they will commit themselves, sacrificially laid upon the altar, determined never to draw back and never to cease their prayers and efforts, assured that they will not labor in vain in the Lord.

Bow down, then, O children of God, ye who are yourselves, as you believe, redeemed by the blood of Christ and renewed by the Divine Spirit, ye upon whom rests the instrumental responsibility of saving souls specially committed to your trust; accept the burden of heaviness and sorrow, as you take their condemnation and peril upon your own hearts. So pray and labor, by the power and in the fellowship of the Spirit working within you, until you prevail.

On the supposition that our fellow-men are in imminent danger of perishing,—and this is the serious truth,—there is no anguish of spirit, no importunity of prayer and effort, too great to be used in their behalf. Surely they cannot strive too earnestly for themselves; and there is no time to delay. The pressure of this burden upon our hearts, let us then confess to each other, and go with it to God, if peradventure he may pour upon us, and upon those dear to us, a blessing which "there shall not be room enough to receive."

# THE OLD FAITH AND THE NEW.

BY REV. GEORGE C. LORIMER.

Stand ye in the ways, and see, and ask for the old paths, where is the good way, and walk therein, and ye shall find rest for your souls.—*Jer.* vi, 16.

TENNYSON sings sweetly, but wildly, "Ring in the Christ that is to be."

Strauss, when nearing the close of his long and laborious life, published a work entitled, "The Old Faith and the New," in which he inquires, "Are we still Christians?" furnishing an elaborate reply in the negative. He declares, writing of a coming religion, "that a new growth will in the future develop itself from the inevitable dissolution of the old." Recently, the Duke of Somerset, in a small work, which breathes something of a nobleman's languidness and superciliousness, sanctions this dreary expectation, saying, "It is now obvious that the theology of former ages cannot be permanently maintained." Of course, it is hardly needful to say that Mr. O. B. Frothingham, and the radical party of America, sympathize with these views, regarding as certain the destruction of the Old Faith, however they may differ among themselves concerning the doctrines of the New. They appear to believe that history must repeat itself, and that as the power of Greek and Roman mythic superstitions was overthrown by the Sophists, so must the essential and distinguishing features of Christianity succumb to the speculative neologists and rationalizing critics of modern times.

As a substitute for what they consider doomed, they offer a variety of speculations, some of which are more radical than others, while all partake of a common inclination towards naturalism and the doctrines of materialism and necessity. The more moderate among them, like some of their ancient prototypes, the Sophists, are not anxious to obliterate the name of the reigning religion, but aim to resolve the so-called mythic tales of miracles into certain great facts and powers of nature, that, as they claim, a more rational ground of support for religious life may be furnished. In this way they think it will be easier to accomplish their ends. They propose to paralyze the heart of the system, and to satisfy humanity with the faint warmth which may survive for a season in the dead body.

Others openly and avowedly are more radical, and agree either with the more extreme among the ancient Sophists, or with the philosophic hopelessness of Epicurus. Justin Martyr wrote of the former class, as it was in his times, "They seek to convince us that the Divinity extends his care to the great whole, and to the several kinds; but not to me and to you, not to men as individuals. Hence it is useless to pray to him; for everything occurs according to the unchangeable law of an endless cycle." And Pliny, speaking from the side of the heathen, declared " that all religion is the offspring of necessity, weakness, and fear. What God is, if in truth he be anything distinct from the world, it is beyond the compass of man's understanding to know."

These and similar views are being revived among us, in connection with modern discoveries in physical science, and the advance in philosophy. We have now Herbert Spencer's doctrine of the Unknowable, by which we are taught that the Unseen Power of the universe cannot be known at all, and therefore cannot reasonably be served, loved, honored, or obeyed. Haeckel, of Jena, and with him many others, regards the course of the world as a ceaseless evolution, implying no plan, choice, or will, on the part of an Unseen Power, and including no choice, will, or moral good or evil, on the part of men; but only a fated cycle of inevitable changes, determined by fixed mechanical laws alone. In this way, according to their statement of the case, " a primitive nebula, called sometimes a fire mist, has developed into worlds, suns, planets, and living things, and will probably return, after countless ages, to nebulous mist, confusion and darkness."

Mr. Frothingham, in one of his published sermons, thus sharply contrasts the fundamental teachings of the New Faith with those of the Old: "The doctrine that man was created perfect, and fell, is contrasted with the doctrine that man was created imperfect, and rose. The doctrine that man was introduced upon the planet a new creature, radically unlike any that had preceded him, is contrasted with the doctrine that man was the natural result of processes that had gone before. The doctrine of the inspiration of the Bible is contrasted with the doctrine of the inspiration of the mind. The doctrine that truth is imparted by supernatural revelation, is contrasted with the doctrine that truth is acquired by patient investigation and slow advance. The doctrine that the soul must be submitted to an external spiritual authority, is contrasted with the doctrine that the soul is itself the seat of authority."

It does not seem to me credible that the world will abandon the religion of Christ for a series of propositions as barren as these. Humanity, though depraved, is surely not inane enough to thrust from it the sources of its intellectual and moral inspiration, and receive instead teachings as unsatisfactory as they are unelevating. I have no fear for the ultimate result of these attacks. Like those which have preceded them at various periods of the past, they will inevitably end in placing Christianity, as believed by the fathers, on a loftier height of influence, and on an impregnable basis of evidence.

But in the meanwhile damage is being done. There are not a few, especially among the youth of our city, whose spiritual future is imperiled. While the conflict rages between the true and the false, while they are measuring strength, the souls of many may be deceived. Christianity is safe enough, but individuals are not. It is this impression that constrains me to look a little more closely than I otherwise should at the teachings of those who desire to be the religious guides of the coming ages.

The Prophet, in my text, commanded the Jews "to stand and see,"—see the foolish ways they were treading,—and return to the old paths." And that the young men, who think for themselves, and who desire to devote their powers to the loftiest of services, may be warned of pitfalls which skeptics and infidels have opened before them, and may have their confidence in the truth and grandeur of Christianity renewed and strengthened, I have concluded, in imitation of Mr. Frothingham, but on the orthodox side of the issue, to present for your consideration:

## THE PERMANENT DISTINCTIONS BETWEEN THE OLD FAITH AND THE NEW.

I. *The Old Faith is Historical, the New is Speculative.* This is a very important distinction, and one very easily understood. If we recur to the ages before Christ's advent, we shall find them setting towards him — on any other hypothesis they are aimless. Not only do prophets foretell his coming, but there are yearnings, as expressed by Plato, and by the Stoics in their dreams of human perfection, which point to him. The voices of oracles, and the inarticulate groanings of the heathen, carry the thoughts of men towards a deliverer. Christ was the goal towards which ancient history set, its meaning and its climax; for since his appearing the great heart of humanity has beat less feverishly and throbbed less painfully.

We all know that since his resurrection he has been the spring and source of the world's mightiest and most wide-sweeping movements. Modern history has been shaped and molded by the mission of Jesus. In China and India, where religion is speculative, stagnation has been the rule for centuries, and they can hardly claim to have had any history during this period. If they are now beginning to stir with new activities, it is because the Cross at last has been planted in the heart of their territory. The West has only escaped this numbed and half-paralyzed condition, because Christianity has been its quickening force.

Christianity is not merely historical as influencing history, but as being in itself historical. Our religion is to be considered first of all as a series of facts. Of course it came rich in ideas; richer than those of the whole body of ancient philosophy, and deeper than those of a Plato or an Aristotle. Nevertheless, its first aspect presents deeds done, events occurring, scenes transpiring in the ordinary relations of life. These are seeds which contain the flower of doctrine. Facts involve truths. Thus the miracles of Christ carried in their train the doctrine of the supernatural, as his resurrection proclaimed the hope of immortality. Indeed, every act of his life, and every movement of his ministry, was pregnant with abstract truth. Nor should it be forgotten that this history formed part of the history of a period, is inseparably interwoven with what for convenience we may call the secular, and cannot be denied without repudiating the annals of the latter as well.

The advantages of this characteristic of our religion are manifold. Not the least is the opportunity it affords for a searching investigation of its claims to superhuman origin. By this we see that it hides behind no veil of mystery, no inexplicable and unintelligible mummeries, but invites the most rigid scrutiny.

To all men it says, "These things were not done in a corner. If you can show that they did not take place as recorded, then the doctrines which are their legitimate outgrowth are unworthy your confidence. Decide the question for yourselves, and just as you would any other in history. Search me, know me, and see whether the facts are not abundantly sustained." Begin your inquiries: Did Christ live? Did he die? Did he rise again? Did he send out the Word, and has it done in the earth what he said it should accomplish? These questions, and others like them, you can readily answer, and with their answer will come acceptance or rejection of the system.

Moreover, there is that in the nature of man which seems to demand this historical element in religion. Few among us, if we may judge from observation, are capable of abstractions. Even the pagans tried to simplify and commend their doctrines by inventing a mythology which gave an appearance of fact to what they taught. We take pleasure in personal existences and their actions. We need an apprehensible object to worship, and if we are to exercise dependence and trust we must have something more before the mind than a vague ideal.

Then such a system furnishes examples—not merely rules and precepts, as speculation does. It shows in the real domain of life what men ought to be. Duty is revealed more clearly, and altogether more attractively. We can idealize with facility, but we execute with difficulty. What we want to feel is that the portrait of human perfection is capable of actualization in such a world as this. It is not the poet's description of purity the heart craves, but the exhibition of it in a life. This is furnished by the historic Jesus, and, in a measure, by the historic apostles. Moreover, there is a consciousness of sin in our hearts. Sin is the most momentous and terrible fact of our experience. We know that it is in the way of our attaining moral excellence, and spiritual perfection. This must be overcome. But how? Not by a dream, a beautiful philosophy, but by a fact equally real and mighty as itself. That fact is supplied by the Cross; and the weary soul, burdened with a sense of its actual guilt, finds there an actual atonement, and actual cleansing. Thus a divine fact is set over against the human fact, and whoever apprehends their relations to each other attains peace of conscience.

On such a foundation as this we can build with satisfaction. Here is a tower firmly constructed, resting on primeval granite, from whose summit we can securely sweep the vast circumference of the spiritual heavens. In comparison with this the foundation on which the New Faith builds is as cloud, mist and fogbank. In exchange for this, we are offered speculations — the surmisings and the hypotheses of modern teachers. Their guesses, their hasty conclusions from uncertain premises, appear to me but miserable substitutes for historic facts.

Speculations are legion. In all circles, evidently, there is a mania in this direction. On all sides there appears to be an intense desire to explain all spiritual phenomena without the aid of Revelation, and as far from its teachings as possible. Science, in the person of its devotees, has become as speculative, as prolific of physico-metaphysical theories as the most bewitched metaphysician could desire. On more than one occasion, distinguished physicists, such as Tyndall and Huxley, have been seen to stray into a perfect wilderness of metaphysics, where, getting enchanted, they have become as enslaved to their physically-named metaphysical entities as some of the Arabian Nights' heroes to the genii. We have had a large, ever-increasing and varied crop of cosmic speculations, ranging from theories of the origin of species to theories of the origin of the universe. Mr. Spencer has tried to build up a science of the universe on a philosophy of the unknowable, which may be embodied in one citation from his pages: "The widest, deepest, and most certain of all facts is that the power which the universe manifests to us is wholly inscrutable."

But after all he has said in support of such a theory, what is it but a bare speculation? And yet men profess to be guided in their thinking by a principle as self-destructive and self-contradictory as this. I say it is both; because if the power behind the universe is inscrutable, how do we know that there is any power at all? How do we know whether it is one or many? And if it is manifest in the universe, it is not wholly inscrutable, and may become clearer and clearer. Professor Tyndall, also, has put forth some memorable speculations, revealing the sweetest simplicity in things historical, and disguising the most airy metaphysics in scientific terms. Witness his Belfast address, the speculative character of which he himself admitted by its subsequent modification.

Then we have assumed theories of development which have not reliable facts by which to verify them. Examples are wanting of man's outgrowth from a lower type. It cannot be proved that he is the latest outcome of Nature's efforts at improving on her own experiments in organic life, or the result of some accidental variety of birth in a chimpanzee family. This can hardly be called a new hypothesis. It was hinted at by very ancient writers. Pliny wrote, "Man is the being for whose sake all other things appear to have been produced by Nature." "Yet," he remarked, "the various kinds of apes offer an almost perfect resemblance to man in their physical structure." Did not this idea find expression in the early pagan mythologies? The god of flocks and herds among the Greeks was represented as a compound creature, having the horns and feet of the goat, and the face of a man. The satyrs also blended the animal with the human. It is to such myths Huxley tries to impart scientific certainty, when he declares "that man has proceeded from a modification or an improvement of some lower animal;" and we are warranted in concluding from his latest array of evidence, that it rests as yet on guesses and inferences, which are only a step removed from those which haunted the imagination of the men who imposed the original myths upon the ancient world.

The same may be alleged of the theories of Comte and Spencer concerning the evolution of religious belief. It is now thought possible to explain the grand ideas of monotheism and of Christian doctrine by the talismanic word "evolution." This is the new "open sesame" to all spiritual mysteries. But the advocates of this speculation furnish no instance of peoples who have grown without foreign influence from atheism into fetichism, and from it through intermediate stages into monotheism; and until such examples be given, hypotheses, claiming to be Natural Histories of Religion, must be judged hypotheses still.

Evolution is much talked of as the solution of the problem of creation, and in some quarters it is regarded as a quietus to the Old Faith. But what does it mean? What does it explain? It is, we are told, a theory of creation. But in what sense? Does it describe the cause or the method? Process is one thing, cause is another. Simplifying the method is not the same as simplifying the cause. Suppose the doctrine is true regarding "the struggle for existence," or the "survival of the fittest,"—still the question remains, Whence came the existence to struggle, the fittest to survive? Whence, after all, came the Nature whose potencies were to accomplish such admirable wonders? The cause, the Supreme cause of all things, is as much in the dark as ever.

Understand me, I do not claim that Mr. Darwin, the author of "Origin of Species," has overlooked this distinction, but others have, and the result is that they have speculated God out of the Universe. The point I make is that the popular metaphysics of science are not warranted by the facts of science, and that speculations only indicate the inability of men's intellect to grapple with the problems of existence, and to provide an adequate substitute for the Old Faith, which they are seeking to supplant.

This limitation has been acknowledged at times by the most thoughtful of the race. Socrates, the most celebrated among the wise men of Greece, designated his knowing that he knew nothing, as that wisdom which he possessed above others. Goethe, the most comprehensive intellect of Germany, says, "Man is an obscure being: he knows not whence he comes, nor whither he goes; he knows little of the world, and, least of all, of himself." "We are all walking amidst mysteries and marvels," says he, in another place; and in Faust:

> "Inscrutable in broadest light,
> To be unveiled by thee she (*Nature*) doth refuse;
> What she reveals not to thy mental sight,
> Thou wilt not wrest from her with bars and screws."

"Nature always contains something problematical, which human faculties are incapable of fathoming." What he says in Faust is no rash exaggeration. There is in the race an insatiable hunger after knowledge, and yet we are compelled to add—

> "That we in truth can nothing know
> This in my heart like fire doth burn."

Pascal declares that "the last step of Reason is to perceive that there are infinitely many things that surpass her, and if she does not attain this knowledge, she is weak indeed." If these opinions are worth anything, they mean that speculation cannot furnish a firm and sure foundation on which to build a religious faith or life. As Goethe says, "Human reason and Divine reason are not the same," and it is only the latter revealed to us that can impart certainty to the beliefs of the former. I spoke of the Christian system a few moments since, as built upon history like a tower for astronomy. May we not now compare it to a lighthouse—while the New Faith in all of its phases is as a ship upon the stormy sea. The vessel that is driving yonder, and the lighthouse, seem both to be built upon the troubled ocean. So the superficial would conclude that the Old Faith as well as the New rest upon the shifting billows of speculation. But in this they are mistaken. Only the New Faith tosses on its uneasy waves; the Old sinks down through them all, through the depths out of sight, and rests upon the adamant of historic verities. Therefore, in that Old tower, lone though it may seem, and exposed to many a storm, I can securely sleep; while worn and spray-blinded the victims of the New, like the fabled Vanderdecken, seeking port for his phantom ship, are driving into the darkness of despair.

II. *The Old Faith is Positive, the New is Negative.* The correctness of this characterization of Christianity cannot be questioned. She has something to say for herself. She is no stammerer. Her speech is distinct, her declarations positive. Rich as well as absolute is her creed. She knows God, and proclaims him in all the circled and full-orbed completeness of his glory. His attributes are defined, his personality declared, and his gracious purposes delineated. The Blessed Christ is not a stranger to her; for the bride knows the bridegroom. His love, tender sympathy, matchless self-sacrifice, and undying faithfulness, are set forth by her in words that burn. The mystery of his nature is unveiled, and "God manifest in the flesh" is the wonderful solution of the problem regarding him, of whom Jean Paul Richter wrote "that with his pierced hands he lifted the gates of Empire off their hinges." To her the significance of his death is not in question. "He died, the just for the unjust, that he might bring us to God," is her inspired explanation. The blood shed on Calvary is in her creed, the bath of cleansing, the fount of renewal. Knowing Christ, Christianity knows the Holy Ghost, who indeed dwells in her and guides her into all truth, comforting and sanctifying her thereby. Clearly she announces the reality of the supernatural, and presents herself as the most distinguished proof; nor does she hesitate to proclaim that every man who sees the kingdom of God must be born from above.

Knowing heavenly things, she knows earthly things as well. She furnishes the only philosophy of humanity — accounting for its origin, its condition, and history. To her unclouded vision eternity is as a world touching upon this. Of heaven she sings, and with no faltering tongue proclaims the deathlessness of the human spirit.

In a word, she supplies a positive, affirmative creed, which, as Napoleon said at St. Helena, "is logical in all of its parts." She does not permit cavil or doubt to trifle with her revelations. Dogmatic and absolute is she on all subjects about which she speaks. To this it may be objected that Christianity is too exclusive and intolerant. But her exclusiveness includes all that we need to know, and her intolerance is simply the sovereignty of truth. Truth cannot admit the possibility of its opposite being true without denying its own authority. Antagonistic views cannot be equally authentic. Were Christianity to cease from declaring herself the only heavenly religion, she would annihilate her power over the conscience, and would even question her own right to exist, for she would be denying her necessity. As it is reported that at the beginning she rejected a place for her Saviour in the Roman Pantheon, so she is compelled by her very nature to reject all alliances and fellowship with other systems. The question of Pilate, "What is truth?" was answered by Christ in the words, "I am the truth;" and in these days his representatives dare not sanction a renewal of heathen skepticism.

How different from this is the New Faith. In its development and in its declarations it is a series of negations. It is a denial. Every step of its melancholy progress reveals this.

About the time of the Reformation a number of uneasy spirits opposed the orthodox doctrine of the Trinity. This movement was expressed by the Italian, Faustus Socinius, who, in 1574, gave up a comfortable position in the Medicean court and betook himself to Germany and Poland, where he became the centre of the denial of the Trinity. Socinianism does not deny either inspiration or supernaturalism, but makes its own subjective notions the standard of all truth. For this reason it rejects the doctrine of Christ's divinity. Wollzogen, the Socinian, said, "It is more credible that a man should be an ass, than that God should be a man."

English deism in the seventeenth century made a still further advance on the path of negation. Lord Herbert of Cherbury (1648) headed the movement, and was followed by Toland, Tindal, Bolingbroke, and others. It was not a frivolous, but an earnest and moral spirit which originated this movement, whose object was to reduce Christianity to general moral and religious principles. Lord Herbert, when he had completed his book, prayed God to show him whether it would be to his glory to publish it. He says, "I had scarcely uttered these words, when a distinct, yet gentle sound, unlike any earthly one, came from heaven. This so supported me and gave me peace, that I considered my prayer as heard." This is wonderful. That God should give direct attestation to a book that denied the possibility of a revelation; and that we are not to believe that he manifested himself in Christ, but are expected to believe that he manifested himself to Lord Herbert of Cherbury, are amiable assumptions, whose logical consistency is not very apparent. Was there ever greater credulity or blindness?

The naturalistic tendency assumed a different form in France. There it was frivolous, immoral, blasphemous, denying the very existence of God. Rosseau, indeed, had some religious feeling, but his delusive theory of a "state of nature" was destructive of everything like religion. Voltaire, whose wit ruled his age, and to whom Frederick the Great wrote, "There is but one God, and there is but one Voltaire," satirized and abused the church, repeatedly saying, "*ecrasez l'infame;*" and he ventured to predict the fall of Christ from his dominion over men's minds in a few decades. Singular infatuation! Jesus yet reigns, and reigns more gloriously than ever, while Voltaire is practically forgotten. Though these men drifted far away from truth, it was reserved for Holbach and his gourmands to touch the bottom of the abyss. In his "Système de la Nature," Baron Holbach affirmed materialism in its baldest form; and denied without scruple the existence of God, the reality of man's spiritual nature, and all ethics, but those of self-love and self-interest.

In Germany, Herman Reimarus, a native of Hamburg, took the lead in religious dissent, and transplanted English deism to the soil of his own country. His polemics were not only against Scripture, but against the morals of Scripture characters, and included Jesus as well. Kant, in his Criticism of Pure Reason, declared all thought to be subjective, and consequently that nothing can be known of the supersensuous in general with objective certainty. God, immortality, are claims of conscience, voiced by this inner witness to truth, and on this foundation he shaped the moral world.

Rationalism, which aims to reduce Christianity to the standard of sound reason, grew out of these elements. It teaches that there is a God, but a God who leaves the world to itself, with the exception of seeing that it does not deviate from the laws he has imposed on it. According to its philosophy, there is not, neither can there be, miracle, prophecy, or direct revelation. God cannot interpose directly, and as to Jesus Christ, he is no miracle, but only, so says this "Daniel come to judgment," the wisest and most virtuous man that ever lived.

Another step in this downward tendency is furnished by Pantheism. It denies the personal God, moral freedom, and the immortality of soul, which Rationalism is supposed to hold. God is cosmical life, or the universal reason in all things. He is not essentially separate from the world. He is, as Spinoza puts it, the ocean of existence, and all things are but waves, ripples, spray, which subside back again into the common life. He is the light, and the various great types of existence are but as the prismatic colors, which are distinct, and yet are but modifications of the one absolute effulgence. There is no personal relation to such a God, because he is impersonal, and has no personal relation to us. Indeed, Hegel taught that he is not self-known, but only known to us; that man is the reality of God, and God merely the truth of man; consequently, while there may be a certain religious disposition, there can be no faith, no hope, no prayer, to such a God. Morality is virtually abolished, for its postulates are destroyed, as there is no deity to impose a law, and no such thing as free will to execute it.

The last step in this dark and chilly descent is Materialism. Feuerbach marks the transition: "God was my first; reason, my second; man, my third and last notion." Thus he expresses the downward course of his theological reasoning. He regards God as a creation of man, and formulizes,—"Man created God after his own image." There is no soul, no freedom, no immortality, nothing but the blackness of night forever.

Here, then, we have the extreme of doubt. It began in denying Christ's divinity; it ends in denying man's spiritual nature, and divinity altogether. It began by revising the piety and morals of religion; it terminates by abolishing them altogether. It can descend no lower. The gospel of earth, the evangel of mud, the millenium of despair has been reached, and lower depth is impossible, save into the abyss profound.

These opinions are misleading many persons to-day — and are the ever-deepening shadows of the New Faith, which envelop mind in the intense darkness of negation. Some of their advocates, to render more plausible their untenable theories, pretend to discard all philosophizing, and set them forth as the doctrine of common sense. The observances of prayer, praise, adoration, faith, hope, are not according to common sense, and are, therefore, useless. The sentiment of religion, God, providence, immortality, are not acceptable to common sense, and must therefore be swept from the mind. But common sense is not infallible. Many other things are contrary to it. Common sense does not justify or explain heroism, the explorer's joy, the reformer's consecration to his work, the saint's rapture, the friend's disinterested loyalty. In a word, common sense, as proclaimed by these gentlemen, simply ignores what is contrary to its earthiness, its sensuousness, and its selfishness.

And this is what is offered as a substitute for the Old Faith. An unknown God, who is also the Untalkable, who is secluded from our prayers, and excluded from our love. Is this common sense? Does common sense demand us to believe that duty is enveloped in everlasting mist, and futurity in impenetrable doubt? Is a huge Perhaps our only anchorage? Are we ever to remain satisfied trying to secure ourselves to a bank of fog, instead of finding some solid rock under whose sheltering strength we can securely rest? Is it common sense to solace ourselves in sorrow with the doctrine of the Uncertain? or to confront the reality of death with a may-be existence to sustain us? Is it common sense to repudiate the deepest and most sacred instincts of our natures, to turn from religion with its blood-bought pardon and its inspirations to purity? Common sense! Rather call it common *non-sense*!

Were the Old Faith burdened with greater difficulties than are alleged against it, were its mysteries deeper, the reason that stirs within us, the conscience that alarms our guilt, the instinct that bids us look beyond the present to a home of cloudless felicity, would rise up in its defense. Man's whole nature pleads for the Old Faith, even as the Old Faith pleads for man. It is light to his spiritual eye, sound to his spiritual ear, life to his death, joy to his spiritual sorrow, hope to his spiritual despair. On its truth he can feed; on its promises he can rest; by its teachings he can guide his feet through this vale of gloom to the Paradise above. He dare not abandon it; he dare not bid chaos come again, or seek strength and peace in that which is without form and void, and on whose dusky waters broods no Heavenly Dove to give it ultimately the order and the glory of a new creation.

III. *The Old Faith is Constructive, the New is Destructive.* With this final distinction, the sphere of the practical is reached. The ultimate test of religious systems must always be identical with that which our Saviour applied to individuals—"fruit." "By their fruit shall ye know them." If the faith which claims to be from heaven is not abundant in good works, if it does not conserve the interests of humanity, elevating and refining, then it lacks the most conclusive of all proofs. The child should resemble the sire. A heavenly faith should be, and will be heavenly. Righteousness, peace, and joy will distinguish it; and only as it answers the real ends of religion in the every-day life of the world will it receive the homage of mind and heart. Nothing to me is so evident as that doctrines emanating directly or indirectly from the Author of creation must be fitted to promote the well-being of society. I can no more conceive that God would make the material world in the interests of his thinking creatures, and then furnish a faith which should work detrimentally or mischievously, than I can believe that sweet and bitter waters proceed from one fountain.

This view of the case has been pretty generally accepted by the representatives of all opinions; and at times has taken shape hostile to the claims of Christianity itself. Not a few of those who advocate the New Faith, have taken pains to show that the Old is evil in its bearings. They have tried to prove that its morality is such that in practice it would dissolve society, disorganize governments, and impede the progress of the race. Strauss accuses it of an unmistakable tendency towards communism, while the communists of France and Germany reject it because of its leanings toward monarchism. Mr. Frothingham, in a discourse on Materialism, declares that evangelical teachers inculcate the following opinions: that "education is of no account; knowledge is worthless; culture is vain; personal goodness counts for nothing; social kindness is valueless; the truest greatness of mind and character is powerless to help man to health and felicity." This is a misrepresentation. The Old Faith encourages the broadest culture, but it denies that it can either regenerate a soul or justify it before God. It proclaims an atonement, not as a substitute for personal training, but as a provision for its reconciliation with the Highest.

But this very conception of an atonement becomes a ground of assault on the morality of the Christian scheme. It is claimed that it justifies injustice, and propounds a theory that subverts every wholesome principle of rectitude. Mr. Frothingham is strikingly severe in his denunciations of this doctrine; and represents it as maintaining that by a material operation the souls of men are to be saved.

He and others fail to see that its inherent and relative morality may be vindicated on such grounds as these: that the very idea of such an atonement has its root in an intense realization of righteousness, moral laxity having nothing to do with it; that no violation of a righteous law is involved, inasmuch as it is appointed and accepted by the lawgiver, and undertaken freely by the substitute; that it is no more unjust, *per se*, that the perfectly holy Christ should die for the guilty as an expiatory sacrifice, than it would be for him to suffer in the slightest degree as an example; and that the avowed end of substitution is not to appease personal feeling in God, but to vindicate righteousness in the inviolable maintenance of law. Neither do our opponents perceive the bearing of the fact, that wherever the atonement is proclaimed it awakens an intense desire for personal purity, renders the conscience more sensitive, and reclaims thousands from vicious courses. Wherever the Old Faith is earnestly, simply, and clearly preached, great revivals follow, thousands are reclaimed and lifted up from despair to hope. When the doctrines of Strauss and Parker result in moral transformations as numerous and as distinct as those which have followed the teachings of Whitfield, Spurgeon or Moody, we shall be more inclined than we are now to credit them with the possession of some redeeming qualities.

The accusations brought by the New Faith are wholly without foundation. Christianity is entirely beneficial. It is constructive, formative. It imparts healthy action to society, having supplied it with its purest ideals and noblest organizations. The dearest interests of the race are conserved by its influence. From it human governments receive their stability, the family its sacredness, industry its honor, law its authority. It has inspired the loftiest sentiments, and kindled the genius of the poet and the artist, while it has bound all ranks in the ties of a noble brotherhood.

The career of the Old Faith, from the past to the present, gives abundant proof of this. Christianity introduced the era of humanity. Not before its advent did men look upon themselves as members of one great family, having a common parentage in the Supreme. Not before were the rights of human personality acknowledged, as sacred and inviolable. Their recognition must be regarded as fruits of Christianity. It made no direct changes in the external arrangements of society when it first appeared; it left laws and privileges, manners and conditions, customs and ranks, as it found them, but it introduced a new spirit into all of these arrangements, which is gradually transforming them to heaven's ideal. It raised the condition of woman from a degraded to an honorable one, declaring that in point of honor there is neither male nor female in Christ Jesus. It made love, which, as Montesquieu says, "at the time of its introduction, bore only a form which cannot be named," the noblest and tenderest power of mental and spiritual life. It created a new family — grounding it in an affection, hearty and genuine, and hitherto unknown.

Not till its dawning did the love for neighbors in any true sense exist. Christianity made the Good Samaritan the pattern of our relations with those from whom we differ in race or creed. By the wondrous mystery and infinite tenderness of the Cross it introduced humanity into the world, and inculcated the virtue of compassion. Care for the sick and poor are of its heart — the spirit of love, of resignation, of self-sacrifice, of its essential genius. It broke down the wall of partition between classes, tribes, and states. Not before did there exist upon earth such a thing as international law, upon which, in our day, the whole frame-work of society depends. Commerce was born of this, and all that we count as progress in the material splendor of nations. She has likewise proclaimed liberty of conscience, and she has added comfort and peace, delivery from the sense of guilt, consciousness of pardon through that ever availing atonement made by Christ for sin. And thus she has become the source of a new and hitherto unknown moral power, the extent of which only the "dateless and irrevoluble circles of eternity" will reveal.

What is more remarkable, Christianity has never done otherwise than promote the wholesome construction of society, whatever may have been its outward conditions, and however it may have tended towards dissolution. During the first centuries, when it celebrated its triumphs in the sufferings of the martyrs, and its rites in the obscurity of the Catacombs, it was only preparing a grander community for the coming Rome. Even in the middle ages, when feudalism and ignorance threatened to end civilization, such as it was, in barbarism, it was Christianity, though obscured by many superstitions, which held the elements of irretrievable disaster in check. At the period of the Reformation, when it appeared that the revolt from superstition might terminate in the destruction of society, the whole movement became a conserving, organizing impulse, from whence modern progress has sprung. During the unhappy war which alienated the sections of our beloved country, it was the Old Faith which prevented absolute anarchy, and the utter wreck of all our institutions. It held us together, and has been the inspiration, if not the formative principle of our reconstruction and present harmony.

The indispensableness of the Old Faith to the order and well-being of society is witnessed to by impartial judges. Montesquieu exclaims: "Wondrous phenomenon! the Christian religion, whose sole object seems to be the happiness of a future life, insures the happiness of the present life." Ziethe calls attention to this saying, and tells of an Indian Prince who desired to know the secret of England's greatness, and to whom Victoria showed neither her splendid army nor navy, but delivered to him a Bible, with the words: "The Word of the Lord is the secret of England's greatness." The well known saying of Goethe is in point, "All epochs under which faith has prevailed, have been brilliant, heart-elevating, fruitful both to contemporaries and posterity. All epochs, on the contrary, in which unbelief, under whatever form, has maintained a sad supremacy, even if for the moment they glitter with a false splendor, vanish from the memory of posterity, because none care to torment themselves with the knowledge of that which has been barren." He adds that French scholars have pointed out the connection of the history of human society with religion, and with the development of the idea of God. Thus Franck (in "Etudes Orientals, 1861,") endeavors to show how the value of a nation's social constitution is proportional to the value of its religious idea. We all know how Castellar traces the glory and stability of the United States to our fathers' faith in the Old Bible. Edgar Quinet, in his lectures at Lyons, (1839,) teaches that "the religious idea is the very essence of civilization, and the formative principle of political constitutions." Benjamin Constant has taken pains to mark the transition to this opinion, and what he says of Quinet will be found true of some others: "He projected his work on religion in the spirit of Atheism,"—note well—"but finished it by seeking the necessary conditions of the existence of civilized society in the religious sentiment." Guizot declares " that all political and social questions always lead to the religious principle for their final solution"; and Proudhon exclaims, " as soon as we go deep into politics, we always stumble upon theology."

These testimonies carry with them the impression that the theories opposed to the Old Faith must be destructive in their tendency — destructive to the moral sense and to the good order of society. What else is inferable from such sentiments as those which pass current among its adversaries? Take the Positivist conception of moral education, which, according to Comte, is the mere knowledge of facts; " of causes of phenomena, whether past or final, we know nothing." According to Mr. Herbert Spencer, children should be made to experience the true consequences of their conduct. Mr. Mill would have inculcated as a leading principle, what he sets forth as true of himself in the sentence, " of direct power over my volitions I am conscious of none." Mr. Bain would have education seek a deliverance from " the whole series of phrases connected with the will," as being " contrived to foster in us a feeling of importance" for which we have no warrant. That is, we are to train our children morally by telling them that there is no such thing as personal freedom or responsibility; that, as Feuerbach would phrase it, " thought is but phosphorous," that "as a man eats, so he is;" and consequently that conduct is but the result of forces over which we have no control, or which is determined wholly by physical qualities.

The premises of the New Faith are necessarily fatal to any remarkable growth of lofty manhood. Contrast them with those of the Old: An indefinable, undiscoverable First Cause is offered the world, instead of a personal and holy God; development of man from a monkey type, instead of creation by the hand of the Highest; phosphorus or protoplasm, or some hidden vital principle, as the source of human action, instead of an undying spiritual essence; atmospheric pressure, or hydrogenic explosions, as the influencing agencies of history, instead of the Holy Ghost; and death and the grave for the race, instead of immortality and the resurrection. Here we have the foundations of the new ethics. But if men are merely creatures of circumstances, if the only laws they are to obey are only those they cannot disobey, if society is the only God they are to worship, and if annihilation is the only destiny they are to anticipate, the moral results of such a barren creed cannot be problematical. It must contract and materialize the nature of man, repress the divine that is in him and foster the animal. Spiritual character, broad, sinewy, strong, can never spring from its teachings. Such men as came of the French Revolution, which was itself, with all of its disorganizing tendencies, a practical phase of the New Faith; or such persons as Mr. R. W. Emerson described, in a lecture on Modern Thought, as "the dapper" product of the new doctrines, are specimens of what they can do in the direction of manhood.

As I think on this subject I cannot but recall a famous passage in the writings of Thomas Carlyle, which suggests a sad illustration of the natural bearing of the New Faith. The grim philosopher quotes from the Moslem myth regarding Moses and the dwellers by the sea. It seems a tribe of men dwelt on the shores of the Dead Sea, and having "forgotten the inner facts of nature, and taken up with falsities, were fallen into sad conditions, — verging towards a certain deeper lake. Whereupon it pleased God to send them Moses, with an instructive word of warning, out of which would have sprung remedial measures not a few. But no; the men of the Dead Sea discovered no comeliness in Moses, listened with real tedium to him, with light grinning, or with splenetic sniffs and sneers, affecting even to yawns — and signified, in short, that they found him a humbug, and even a bore. Moses withdrew. The men of the Dead Sea, when we next went to visit them, were all turned into apes. They sat on trees, grinning in the most *un-*affected manner, gibbering and chatting very genuine nonsense. The Universe has become to them a humbug. Only every Sabbath there returns to them a bewildered half-consciousness, half-reminiscence, as they look out through those blinking, smoke-bleared eyes of theirs, that they had a soul once. They made no use of their souls, and so have lost them."

To me this is a tragical picture of the tendency of the New Faith. The blessed realities of the Gospel are rejected, and men, taught to sneer at their own spirituality, degenerate towards the ape species. They chatter or mew unmusically regarding nature, theories of evolution, or positive philosophies, and have only a dim consciousness of something they once had, which is now forever gone. Their soul is lost to them. And we may rest assured that apes, with their screeching and chatter, cannot give such a society as enlightened Christian men can create.

Those who expect otherwise are fatally deluded. When not put to the strain, when not tested by the trials of life, the new doctrines may not seem to be injurious, but they will prove so in the long run, to the individual, and to society as well. You may remember the fate which overtook Donaldson and a companion, in 1876. At first the balloon, to which they committed themselves, rose majestically in the calm, but after a little while the storm struck it, and it was driven wildly over land and lake. Through the darkness of that night, through the battle in the clouds, they were borne, only to perish. Neither came back, and only the dead body of the youth, washed ashore by the lake, gave clew to the mystery.

Now, there are spirits as reckless as these adventurers, who claim that evil effects can not overtake them, whatever doctrines may be received, so long as they are sincere. In this apprehension they are wofully mistaken. They forget that Donaldson and his associate were perfectly sincere in believing that they could navigate the aerial ocean in safety, and yet their sincerity did not preserve their frail vessel from the fury of the storm. And if they hold on to a bag of gas, to an inflated theory, when the storm tries it, as we are not living in a world of shams, but of realities, they will be dashed to pieces. The men in the balloon were never in a position of more peril, than are those who would rise heavenward in some frail machine of their own constructing, instead of ascending the mystic ladder revealed by Christ, which leads man directly to holy fellowship with his God.

CONCLUSION.—To what I have written it may be answered, the human mind is so constituted that it craves new ideas, and new theories. It cannot satisfy itself with the thoughts and beliefs of the past; it demands fresh conceptions for the future. There is beyond question an error in this representation. What the mind really needs is something true, not something new; and in the true, however old, will be ever found its most nourishing aliment. If I hand you a rose fresh from the garden, dyed in nature's richest colors, and fragrant with the rarest perfume, with dew-drops glistening like diamonds on the leaves, will you toss it away contemptuously, exclaiming, "the eye requires something new?" Surely not. In the realm of the beautiful there is really nothing new. Its forms may be re-produced in various ways, its outlines and expression may be copied by the art of the sculptor or the painter; but they are as immutably fixed as the laws of right and wrong. The fluidity or changeableness of the beautiful is only apparent; in fact, whether in nature, in marble, or in canvas we look for it, we look for the definite and immutable properties which reveal themselves in a flower, and without which the object contemplated would not be beautiful at all. When the eye craves satisfaction, it is seeking for these permanencies; and when they are found, it has nothing more to seek for. Not the newly beautiful, but the truly beautiful is its delight. This principle is as applicable to the spiritual sight as to the eye. That within man which yearns for religion, can only be satisfied with that which corresponds to itself, and that which thus corresponds must abide; for were it to fluctuate or change essentially, it would cease to be adapted to the end for which it has been instituted.

A new religion is no more required by the race,

than a new world. The sun that shines on us shone on our sires, the stars that gleam upon our way gleamed on theirs. Old ocean throbs no differently for us than it did for them; the winds sigh now as in former ages, day and night succeed each other, and the flowers come and go as through the centuries which never can return. I love the old world—the old earth and the old heavens, because they are old. To me they are made peculiarly sacred by the thought that they surrounded the sages, poets, heroes and martyrs of the past. I tread the dusty roads they trod, I behold the scenes which charmed them or inspired them. I hear the sounds which broke upon their ear and chased away their sense of solitude. Dear earth! the footprints of the noble are in thy bosom; their tears fell upon thee, and thou dost treasure them in thy secret places; their sighs mingled with thy solemn moanings, and thou dost whisper them beneath the heavens; and their struggles and their triumphs stormed across thee, and though they have left many a scar upon thy wondrous face, they have left an undying glory too.

Equally as precious, because equally sufficient for all our needs, is the Old Faith. Generations of the best, of the purest, of the truest, have believed its doctrines, rejoiced in its promises, breathed its prayers, hoped for its victories, and died in its assurances of eternal felicity. Thus let us live, hope and rejoice, until that bright day shall dawn when the immortal shall be translated from the old realm of faith to the new realm of sight:

> "For when at last, from life's dark road,
>   We climb heaven's heights serene,
> All light upon the hill of God
>   In God's light shall be seen.
>
> All kingdoms of the truth shall there
>   To tearless eyes be shown;
> And, dwelling in that purer air,
>   We'll know even as we're known."

# LEARN OF ME.

### BY GEORGE ZABRISKIE GRAY, D.D.

Take my yoke upon you, and learn of me; for I am meek and lowly in heart: and ye shall find rest for your souls. — *Matt.* xi. 29.

AT the feet of many masters have the children of men sat to gain wisdom, as the centuries have been rolling by. With each succeeding age has the number of those masters been increasing, for, in this noble quest, do men not only learn of those whose voices they may hear, but, allowing no lapse of time to rob them of their teachers, they sit at the feet of the dead, as well as of the living. Accordingly, to-day, when the throng of learners is greater than it has ever been before, is the number of teachers greatest. In every land, do countless students listen not only to those who lend such glory to the present age, they also bow before the utterances of those whose wisdom these later years inherit; those, whose names, like monuments, mark the stages of the onward movement of mankind.

But there is one teacher who makes claim to a greater deference than we dare give to these. Though it is long since he lived on earth, he speaketh still, and speaketh as does none other whose articulate voice is silent. Through a church founded by him to this end, and enduring while the nations rise and fall, through a volume that embodies his instructions, and which is the only perfect record of any teacher's wisdom, Jesus cries to-day, as he has ever cried: "Learn of me!" Over every scene of study, in university or school, in crowded halls or secluded rooms, to all who are engaged in the pursuit of truth, does his voice ring out: "O, ye children of men, whatever knowledge ye are seeking, whatever guides ye follow, be not content therewith! Come to listen unto me, for I can teach you that which is better still: that which I alone can impart, and that without which all your labor is in vain!"

And who is this Jesus that makes such a supreme claim upon our discipleship? It is a daring thing to demand a higher allegiance than we give to all others, however wise or good they be. But it is not more daring than other claims he makes. This same Jesus said: Love me! obey me! trust me! "I am the resurrection and the life. He that liveth and believeth in me shall never die!" "I, if I be lifted up, will draw all men unto me." "He that loveth father or mother more than me is not worthy of me." "I am the light of the world. He that followeth me shall not walk in darkness, but shall have the light of life." In such and many other like passages, we behold what has been called a "sublime egotism," which demands that upon the speaker be concentrated all the obedience, all the affection, all the homage of men. But, who ventures to ask this at our hands? We are made for God, and for a God who will not give his glory to another. We should not, and we will not, enshrine in our hearts any being but our Maker. No one less than he is entitled to our adoration, and no one less than he shall have it. And no one that ever trod this earth, save Jesus, has asked it. There has never been a sage or prophet who has claimed such prerogatives, because they have all known that, to draw men to themselves, is to draw them away from God. Therefore, when we find Christ advancing such a claim, which no one else has advanced, and which only Deity has the right to advance, we must either believe that he was the greatest foe of all that is proper as regards our moral obligations, or that he had the right to call our hearts to himself because he is our God. The former alternative is something that we cannot admit regarding one so holy. Consequently, this "sublime egotism" compels us to confess him divine. Convinced, then, that in him the Deity dwelt incarnate, because we cannot believe him such a rival of that Deity as he otherwise must be, we, who follow him, sit humbly at his feet to learn of him. And this is the reason why he demands your discipleship, and your supreme allegiance. His being your Lord and your God renders disregard of him folly. Confining your study to other words than his, is self-robbery, and a squandering of the few days wherein you must grow wise, not only for time, but for eternity.

And what will Jesus have us learn of him? Did he come to teach us regarding worldly science? No; herein he interferes not. He leaves us to investigate for ourselves, save that he expects that what he has revealed of God's ways and workings be accepted as fundamental truth. To this extent, we must subordinate even our secular studies to his utterances. By these disclosures, we must test the accuracy of every conclusion that has any connection with the great questions of creation and of providence.

But, in the sphere of moral truth, Jesus asserts his exclusive claim as a teacher. Here, our study must be begun, continued, and ended in him. His precept that we are to learn of him signifies that we are herein to prosecute our search with constant reference to him, and in the light of his doctrine.

Let us briefly notice, now, what he teaches in this moral sphere; what it is that we are to learn of him, and of him alone. And, first, we will notice two points which are more nearly connected with the immediate idea of the text.

He teaches *what our characters should be.* "Learn of me, for I am meek and lowly in heart." Now, this is not the ideal of character which accords with the usual human standards, much less that which was admired in the days when he lived. We are apt to think, and society demands, that we should be the reverse, quick to assert ourselves and prompt to resent indignity. We must be ready to vindicate what is called our honor, and retaliation is regarded as proper and becoming. Without this spirit, not a few will call us cowards, and the world will be apt to tread upon us. The duel is widely viewed as the highest expression of this trait. It is regarded as something noble and chivalric, even by many who would not resort to it. He who seeks revenge in its deadly risk wins envy, and by it is allowed to secure oblivion for almost any disgrace.

Nor is this spirit of meekness and lowliness one that promotes the acquisition of the aims that men usually seek: wealth, or fame, or station. It is apt to stand in the way of such advance, since it permits the self-asserting to push on when such a character would pause.

Yet, in the face of the world's idea of manliness and honor, in the face of what is required by the world's competition, Jesus tells us to be meek and lowly. He teaches that this is the truest and loftiest character — the one we should seek to acquire.

But, is it not so? Think of the result of the adoption of this spirit! Would it not be a blessing to mankind? Should we not, by living up to it, be able to do more to brighten earth than can be done by those whose standard is that other spirit, which the world admires, and which is so natural to its devotees? If a rule of life can be tested by its usefulness and power, surely then this one, of which we are speaking, must rank, as Jesus placed it, higher than its reverse, attractive as the latter may seem at first glance. To be quick to forgive is nobler than to be quick to resent, and bravery to be kind is a better example than bravery to retaliate.

But the truth of this is seen, best of all, in the contemplation of Jesus himself. Where has there been a character like his? On whose head do men place such crowns of loveliness as upon his own? What memory is invested with such a spell? Who has done as much as he, to provoke imitation through the ages that have gone? Who does not confess that, in this sense at any rate, his is the "name above every name?" Yet, this is all because he was meek and lowly of heart. That is the secret of his isolated glory among the sons of men, and the homage paid him shows that, whatever be the world's idea of manliness, it yet confesses that its noblest, fullest embodiment demands a different spirit than that of pride. Will you not then, you who are young, act upon this, and remember that the life of him, whom you confess to be the type of manhood, proves meekness to be the crown of character, and humility the sublimest rule of action? For he, "when he was reviled, reviled not again; when he suffered, he threatened not."

And, again, Jesus teaches *what our lives should be*. The form which our careers should assume is the great question that meets us at the outset. Generally, the ideal and hope that are cherished are eminence and fame. To be conspicuous, or what is called great, is the end for which all is shaped, and the desire that provokes the efforts of the young. But the Great Master shows and tells us that our lives should be the outflow of the character which he taught. Meekness and lowliness of mind will produce living, not unto self, but for God and man. That is, they will result in a life, which, like his own, is consecrated to do the Father's will. In this way, should we mould our days, making them the fulfilment of a mission, wherein we tell of God while we grow like him.

But, at once it is replied that this will not lead to success, will not gain us wealth or station. Yet, what is success? Is it not to succeed in that for which life is given, and for which we are made? And is not this to be done in living as Jesus taught?

Yet, even in this same sense of gaining the attention and admiration of our fellow-men, this is the surest mode of attaining success. Earth ranks its saints above its heroes, and makes shrines of the tombs of those who blessed it, rather than of those of the sages that taught it. And thus has it occurred that many a man and many a woman have made the world ring with their names, by living consecrated lives, who would have been unknown and forgotten, had they pursued the aims that usually dazzle the mind of youth and lead on the steps of age.

But we are to live such a life, not because of this, but because of more intrinsic reasons, and because he who came to teach us herein has so willed it. He says it has the highest claims, and to see what it is in its fullness, he tells us to learn from his example.

For, in both these respects of which we are speaking, there is one reason why Jesus alone can teach us. To learn what character and life should be, we need more than precept, we require example. Without this, all words are vain. The most perfect delineation of what we should be, though given from heaven, would be ineffective to guide us, without an illustration in one who realized it. This is what we find in Jesus. Where else may we look for example but to him? He alone realizes the ideal of humanity, and his career alone teaches us what our own should be.

On the plain of Baalbec, beneath the snowy peak of Hermon, there lie scattered the fragmentary relics of a vast structure, which formerly rose there in beauty. There are crumbling walls and shattered arches, and, among them, are seen countless columns, which, once lofty and graceful, are now all either broken or prostrate — all save one. That one still stands, erect and perfect as when the chisel last touched it, wielded by forgotten hands. And, as from the side of Lebanon, the traveler looks down upon that wide Syrian plain, that isolated pillar, rising so grandly above the universal ruin of its fellows, long detains his gaze. It seems the more perfect, because it is so solitary, and it reminds him of what the temple must have been, of which it is the sole relic that has survived the earthquake and the storm. So it is that, as we look out upon the plain of life, which lies outstretched beneath the throne of God, we see but universal ruin, but the wreck of the temple of humanity. All the lives that compose it are shattered and fallen, save one. One, and only one, form rises perfect amidst the scene; only one is untouched by the storms and catastrophes of sin; only one tells what man was and what man should be. And that is the form of Jesus of Nazareth. It is this that renders him the only teacher who can show us how to live, the only one to whom we can go to learn lessons as of a faultless model.

But it will not do to stop here in speaking of what Jesus inculcates. There are those who are fond of exalting him as a teacher, and describe him, in this light, in terms of admiration to which he is justly entitled, but who, nevertheless, by a strange inconsistency, ignore the great burden of his instruction and are oblivious of the chief end of his mission. For, to teach us regarding life and character, of which we have spoken, was but a secondary object with him. It were but a partial view of his work to confine our thoughts thereto; so partial as to be false and misleading. His great teaching was that he is the Saviour of sinners, and that he came to redeem men by dying for them. There are no more frequent or plainer declarations than those to that effect. "As Moses lifted up the serpent in the wilderness, even so must the Son of Man be lifted up, that whosoever believeth in him should not perish, but have everlasting life." "The Son of Man is come to give his life a ransom for many." Most clearly was this expressed in the establishment of the sacrament by which he was to be remembered. Of the bread, he said: "This is my body, which is broken for you"; of the wine: "This is my blood of the New Testament, which is shed for you and for many, for the remission of sins." That is, this rite shows us the light in which he desired to be thought of, forever; not as a teacher, but as a Redeemer, who died for men, that their sins might be forgiven upon the basis of that death. To secure for them, in this way, pardon and life eternal, was the aim of his incarnation.

Let this sink deeply into your minds and hearts, my friends. If you would learn of him who so rightly calls you to listen to him, you must accept this, his supreme doctrine. If you would make him your

Master, you must make him your Saviour. It is a mockery of him to pretend to be taught by him, while you accept but the lesser, and reject the greater, truth he seeks to impart. Take in all his teaching, and thus will you know how to live here, and how to gain life hereafter.

And, in closing, Jesus says regarding all his teaching, that by it "you shall find rest for your souls," or, as we may also read it, "repose for your lives." This is what renders it the best of all learning, and makes it true that there is no wisdom like that which he gives. For, rest is what we need more than anything else, in a world like this. Peace of mind, calmness, fearlessness of what surrounds us, and of what is before us, serene superiority to anxiety — this is the most precious of acquisitions for you and me. Above all, is this precious in the crises of life, the emergencies which its vicissitudes bring. Yet, nothing can give this but the teaching of Jesus. Other learning has its value and its pleasures. It can do much for us when the skies are clear and when all is well. But it can do nothing for us when the skies are clouded, when the heart is heavy and the dark mountains are near. For, such days must come, sooner or later, to all of us; days when life's burdens are heavy and its cares severe; when sickness enfeebles the frame, or bereavement endues every landscape with gloom; when the brightness of earth is gone, and, of all its gifts, the heart says: "I have no pleasure in them" —

days, when age has whitened the hair and bowed the once vigorous form; when eternity is close at hand and the great veil begins to rise, so solemnly, for us to pass through. In such days, what other teachers shall have told you will have no more the charm it may now possess; you will no more pursue with interest what had erst led you so alluringly onward. Only that will then be prized which will enable you to endure, and keep your souls at rest. And that is what Jesus tells us of himself and his salvation.

Therefore is all preparation for life incomplete and inadequate which does not include such learning. It is vain for you to imagine you are qualified for the experiences you must meet, if you are not a disciple of Christ. You are, in this case, but advancing to sorrow, challenging adverse circumstances but to be defeated, going out but to encounter trials wherein you will have no peace. But, begin at once to study the Gospel, wherein your Saviour's words and work are so perfectly recorded, and there will you gain all that he imparts to those who submit to his instruction. Do this, and you will find, as others have found who have trodden life's stern path before you, that, in coming years, when care and disappointment have taken away the halo of the gilded present, you will hold as the dearest and the best, not the knowledge you will have received from human masters, but that which you will have learned at the feet of Jesus.

# THE SEPARATION OF THE SOUL FROM GOD.

### BY W. F. MALLALIEU, D. D.

Behold, the Lord's hand is not shortened, that it cannot save; neither his ear heavy, that it cannot hear. But your iniquities have separated between you and your God, and your sins have hid his face from you, that he will not hear.—*Isaiah* lix. 1, 2.

I ASK your serious and prayerful attention to these three thoughts derived from the text:

1. The separation of the soul from God;
2. The causes of this separation; and,
3. The consequences of such separation.

It is seen at once that it is impossible for the soul to be separate from God, in the sense of being remote or distant from him. God is omnipresent, and wherever the soul may be, still God is there. God is in the heights of heaven, and in the depths of hell; he is in the uttermost parts of the earth, and the most distant island of the sea; and if the soul could flee away forever on the wings of the morning, it could never escape the surrounding presence of God. He is not only everywhere, but he fills immensity, so that the universe and all space is pervaded with God. Immensity, and space, and distance, are all alike to him, who, in the perfection of his nature, surrounds all space and fills every point, without absence and without change.

More than this, God is present to know and remember, for the purposes of judgment and retribution, the unhallowed thoughts, and words, and deeds, of every soul of man. If there be any place in all the universe where men are inclined to believe that God cannot enter, it is the silent, secret chambers of the soul. Because it is possible to conceal our inmost thoughts from our fellow-men, we are inclined to think they may be concealed from God; because we can shut ourselves up within ourselves and keep the world outside, we may and do sometimes fancy that we can close the approaches of the soul to God.

But the real truth is, God is so near to us, and is so watchful of all we do, that we never perform an action, however slight it may be, without the direct cognizance of God. And from the first word we ever lisped up to the last utterance of our lips, whether those words have been words of love or strife, whether of complaining or thanksgiving, whether of cursing or blessing, every word we have ever uttered has been heard of God, and they are all remembered.

The worst part of every one's life is in his thoughts. No one has ever done as wickedly as he has thought.

The last thing that any one of us would wish to have made known to the world would be the thoughts which have been in our minds since first we were conscious of thought. Men cover them up and keep them out of sight, and repress them, and to a very great extent conceal them, and they sometimes imagine that there is no being in the universe that knows anything about what is going on within the innermost soul. Men turn down the lights, or put them out altogether, draw the curtains, and close tight the shutters, and sit down with their thoughts in the darkness. They know that no angel can enter and intrude upon their privacy, that no human being living or dead can reach them in their seclusion, and they dream that they are alone. But they forgot when they closed the doors, and put out the light, and drew the curtains, and closed the shutters, that God was inside with them all the time, and they forgot that the darkness and the light are alike to him; and there he is in the very secret place of the soul, and he knows every thought, and knows it with all the infinite perfection of his omniscience, and knows it to remember it, and knows it to approve or to condemn.

O that this solemn, awful thought might abide with us, that God is absolutely and constantly near to every soul, searching our hearts, and knowing us better even than we know ourselves.

Hence we see that the separation of the soul from

God, which is spoken of in the text, is not that of distance, but rather a moral separation. The soul that is separate from God is unlike God in the very nature and essence of its moral constitution.

God is a being of infinite purity and holiness. In him there is not the slightest stain of impurity in any respect, there never has been in all the eternity of the past, and there never will be in all the eternity that is to come. From everlasting to everlasting, this freedom from all impurity has been, and will be, the distinguishing characteristic of God. It is also true of him that there is no degree of imperfection which attaches itself to the divine nature. Purity is possible, and still there may not be absolutely no imperfection. Of God alone can it be said that he is absolutely and infinitely perfect in all the attributes of his nature. "In him there can be no malice, or envy, or hatred, or revenge, or pride, or cruelty, or tyranny, or injustice, or falsehood, or unfaithfulness; and if there be anything besides which implies sin, and vice, and moral imperfection, holiness and purity, as applied to God, signify that the divine nature is at an infinite distance from it."

But it is not sufficient to say of God that he is devoid of all impurity, and all imperfections, and all unholiness, for this is but a negative statement of the facts in the case. It is equally true that God is infinitely pure, and perfect, and holy. In all his volitions, in the exercise of his compassion, his mercy, his pity, his goodness, his wisdom, his faithfulness, his justice, and in every other namable and unnamable attribute of his nature, and in the very essence of his nature, he is infinitely pure, and perfect, and holy; and this to such a degree, and in such an absolute sense, that we cannot express it in human language, nor fathom the fullness of its significance, though we were possessed of the sublimest intellect ever created in earth or heaven. Now, then, when we find a soul that is unlike God in these respects, we shall find one that is separate from him.

There is no uncreated being but God in the universe, and there can be no other being that is infinite in all his perfections; in this sense there will always be an infinite distance between the created and the uncreated. But in respect to purity and holiness, we may readily perceive that the creature may possess these qualities. If he does possess them, then he is near to God and God is near to him. But the sad truth is that man is fallen and he does not manifest these characteristics. He is impure in his thoughts, and perverse in his volitions. His heart is full of envy, and malice, and pride, and revenge, and cruelty, and lust, and falsehood, and unfaithfulness, and of every evil passion, propensity and desire, so that the very sources of thought and feeling and action are thoroughly corrupt and unholy.

The result is, that the soul in its nature is removed from God almost as far as the east is from the west, and it is a wonder of mercy and love and power that ever a reunion can be effected. The separation spoken of in the text not only involves this unlikeness of nature, but also an equally great dissimilarity in the things that are loved by God and the soul.

God loves everything that is pure and holy and good, and he hates whatever is not. He loves righteousness, and goodness, and virtue, and truth, and integrity, and everything that is excellent, and hates the opposites; while the soul that is separate from God hates all those things that God loves, and loves all the things that God hates. Nor may we wisely flatter ourselves that these things are not true of fallen human nature, for there are the best reasons for supposing that it takes the fear of punishment, the restraints of society, and the gracious influences of the Spirit of God to prevent the turbulent passions of depraved hearts from blasting with the hot breath of hell, even to utter destruction, every loving and holy thing that glorifies redeemed humanity.

II. We come now to inquire as to the causes of this separation of the soul from God.

I love to think of every new-born child, of every little babe, that it is very near to God. I am glad for the faith I have that "heaven lies all about us in our infancy." I believe that it is true that each little child is "a new, sweet blossom of humanity, fresh fallen from God's own home to flower on earth."

Whatever may have been the ruin of the fall, and the corruption of the race, the all-embracing work of Christ for the salvation of mankind has put all children into a position where the Saviour himself might say of them, "Suffer the little children to come unto me and forbid them not, for of such is the kingdom of God."

Our first parents were near to God. They held intimate personal communion with him. He daily revealed himself to them amid the bowers of Eden. There was no sense of separation from God felt by the sinless pair. But the tempter entered that abode of purity and love, and in an evil hour temptation was yielded to, and the holy and righteous law of God was violated, and sin entered the world. How great the change! God was no longer a welcome and desired visitant, but the guilty ones fled from his presence and hid themselves in the vain purpose to put themselves where God could not find them. In their loves and hates, in their natures, all had changed, and sin had caused the change — sin had separated them from God.

Now, whatever theory of the effects of the fall one may adopt, the first sin of childhood leaves us amid surroundings which, if yielded to, will draw us more and more away from God. Every added sin increases the distance, until we find that the moral separation between the soul and God is but little short of an impassable gulf, and it would be impassable forever had it not been bridged by the infinite grace of the Lord Jesus Christ.

The effect of sin upon the soul is of the most destructive character, and perhaps in no respect is it more clearly seen than in the fact that it separates the soul from God. God is the source of all the good that any of his creatures ever enjoy. All mercies, gifts and graces come from him, and every sin indulged in separates us further and further from this inexhaustible source of blessing. Every year, every day, every hour we become more and more unlike God in all the attributes of our moral nature; we gradually lose our sympathy for his plans and purposes, and come at last to despise his law, and then we hate the Lawgiver, and our rebellious wills rise up, and we say in our hearts and actions, if not in words, we will not have him reign over us.

It is said that a celebrated painter once wished to portray upon canvas the contrast which exists between innocence and guilt as manifest in the countenance of a little child and a hardened, imbruted criminal.

After diligent search he found a little child which seemed to him the most beautiful and perfect embodiment of purity and innocence he had ever seen. Its form was faultless; its wavy tresses kissed by the sunlight were perfect; its complexion was clear and rosy;

its eyes were large and lustrous; its lips were perfect in outline and overflowing with sweet prattling words; its forehead was full, broad and white; in fact, every feature, as well as the complete expression, was radiant with almost more than mortal loveliness.

With the greatest care the painter transferred the face to his canvas and hung it up in his studio until he should find its opposite.

For years he sought in all directions for a face that should comprise everything hideous and hateful. He went among the poorest and the outcast of great cities; he visited the haunts of infamy and vice for a face that should form a perfect contrast to that of the little child. Success at last crowned his efforts, for with true artistic delight he one day discovered in a prison a face which completely met his ideal. It was the face of a felon chained to the floor of the dungeon, where, for the most appalling crimes, he was to be confined until his trial. He was young in years and yet he looked like an old man, for his form was bowed and tremulous, the result of unbridled debaucheries; his hair and beard were long, and matted, and filthy; his lips were purple and swollen, and his mouth was full of cursing; his eyelids were corroded, and his eyes were bleared and bloodshot; his brows were coarse, and rough, and long; his forehead was wrinkled and furrowed with deep lines of sin and shame; in short, the face was that of a young man who, by a career of vice, had destroyed his manhood and made himself as hideous to behold as though he had been taken possession of by a legion of devils.

In due time the painter prepared for his work, but strange to tell, ere the task was accomplished he learned that the young man before him was the identical person whose childish portrait he had kept hanging in his studio for so many years.

It was sin that had separated this young man from his pure, sweet, holy childhood; it was sin that had swept him out, away from his mother's arms, and his home of love, and his hopes of life and heaven, out into the storm, and the darkness, and the horrible tempests of lust and crime, until he was as far from his own cradle-innocence as the flame-encircled gates of hell are far away from the glorious pearly portals of the city of God.

Just this terrible effect sin will have upon the soul if it be cherished in any heart. It obliterates all lines of spiritual beauty; it destroys the moral likeness of the soul to its Creator; it causes the soul to become more and more like the lost and rebellious spirits which once shone in brightness and purity before the throne, but are now sunk to the utter depths of hopeless wreck and ruin; it crowds the soul away from light and life and joy, away from the Cross and the Crucified, into the outer blackness and midnight of despair; it separates the soul from God.

I know the unconverted, surrounded by all the gracious influences of Christian society, and still susceptible to the powerful attractions of Calvary, may be inclined to say that the sins they have committed cannot cause such a complete separation from all good. But why not? All sin, when it is finished, bringeth forth death. The nature of all sin, its real essence, is the same; it is a refusal to do the will of God.

Suppose you do not swear; suppose you are not dishonest; suppose you have not broken the letter of one of the Commandments of the Decalogue; suppose for the sake of friends, and children, and other relatives, and for your own sake, you have so conducted that no blemish has ever rested upon your character, and you have gained and now enjoy the confidence of all who know you: it does not therefore follow that you are united to God, and that you dwell in him, and that he abides in you. With all this, in your hearts you may be rejecters of God. You may be neglecters of his Word; you may turn away from the inspired volume and deny its claims, without ever having given a single week of all your lives to the serious and sober investigation of those claims.

You may rest assured that such a course as this will separate your souls from God. It may not be your deliberate purpose to cut yourselves loose from the divine and heavenly attractions, but still I pray you to understand that no surer method of doing so can be taken than that you are pursuing.

Perhaps I am appealing to some not guilty of outbreaking sins, who are nevertheless indulging in some passions, desires, or ambitions, which are opposed to fellowship with God. Each one must know just what the difficulty is, and it is manifest that it is the very thing which in time past has kept you from God. You may love riches, and are too eager to gain them to be strictly honest; you love worldly pleasures, and you know not how you can give them up, and yet you know that you must sacrifice them or you can never come into sweet communion with your Heavenly Father; or you may be cherishing wrong feelings; there may be pride, or wrath, or revenge, or envy, or malice, in your heart, and while this is so you know your prayers even are all in vain, and yet you refuse to yield to your convictions of right and duty, while all the time you are drifting away from God. These evil propensities and passions of the unregenerate nature have a terrible affinity with the spirits of darkness and death, and they will drag down to perdition any soul who clings to them.

O, my unconverted readers, why will you not to-day bring out these idols which keep you from God and his love, and destroy them. Say to pride, and anger, and wrath, and malice, and envy, and revenge, "Ye shall be dethroned, ye shall die;" say to the lust for vain and sinful pleasures, and to the greedy desire for gain, "Ye too shall die;" say to carelessness, and indifference, and sloth, and every rebellious feeling of the heart, "Ye too shall die;" and then from the very depths of your souls, cry out—

> "Nearer, my God, to thee; nearer to thee,
> E'en though it be a cross that raiseth me."

And I tell you, you shall feel a glorious thrill of joy filling your souls as you realize that the sins which separated you from God, and the iniquities that hid his face from you, have all been pardoned, and you are resting in the divine love.

III. What are the consequences of this separation from God?

First of all, the spiritual life of the soul is extinguished, and insensibility and death ensue.

It is not many years since I accompanied a young man to the Boston and Maine depot, as he was about to leave the city for his distant home in the country. Coming here when a boy only thirteen or fourteen years of age, one of a large family of children, and with a very scanty wardrobe, and scarcely more money than enough to bring him to the city, he soon found himself without means, without employment, and without friends. But he would not be discouraged, for he had come from his rural home to seek his fortune, and with visions of future wealth as the inspiration of his soul. Day after day he spent in looking for a situation, and night after night he slept in a hogshead, in which was a little straw, until at length he secured a place as errand boy in a retail store.

A more diligent and faithful boy was never known; early and late he toiled, and soon gained the good-will of his employers, and was rapidly advanced, until, in a few years, he was admitted to the firm, with every prospect that the dreams of his youth would be realized. But, by improper exposure, he took cold; the cold was followed by a cough; then came debility and emaciation. Kind friends warned him of his danger at every step of the disease, and well do I remember that many a time, in his store and elsewhere, I urged him to leave his business, and take the rest and recreation he so much needed, only to be answered, with a pleasant smile, that he was young and strong, and that the little cold that was troubling him would soon be gone; he would drive it off, and all would be well. But it was not to be conquered in this way, and so it went steadily on its course. Strength was gone, and appetite was gone, and vigor and elasticity were gone, and with a sad interest I saw him tearfully leave the place where, for half his life-time, he had toiled to win the success he had so ardently desired. Only a few days after and I saw him in the cars, and as I left him I put my arms around his neck, and bade him a last farewell; for I knew I should see him no more on earth, for he was even then a dying man, just able to go home to his father and mother, that he might look once more on the familiar scenes of his childhood, and then let the loved ones close his eyes and bury him in the quiet village grave-yard. Before he would take rest, or use the proper remedy, or consult the skillful physician, he had gone so far that all human hands were too short to reach and save him, and however full of sympathy may have been the hearts of his many friends, yet all his appeals for help must have been without avail.

He did, in regard to his bodily health, just what so many are doing in regard to their spiritual well-being. In his case, death was the consequence of his neglect; and so the soul that separates itself from God by outbreaking sin, or by carelessness and indifference, will find, when it is all too late, that the soul must die outside the reach of the boundless mercy and love of God.

Again, the soul that is separate from God will miss forever the eternal revelation which God will make of himself to all who love him. In all the realms of thought and being, there will be to the outcast sinner no manifestation of the divine benignity. He may gaze Godward, but never will he see light, never a smile of recognition, never an uplifting of the clouds and darkness that hide the awful throne of the majesty of God.

The saved will see Christ, and his glory will be shared by them; they will find in Christ the eternal satisfaction of every immortal aspiration; they will walk with him in white, and join with cherubim, and seraphim, and angels, and archangels, in the peans of love and victory that all heaven is waiting to hear, and which will be heard throughout the universe, even to the depths of the nethermost hell, when all the saints are safely gathered to their eternal home.

The last revelation of Christ to the soul that is separated from God will be that of the judgment seat, when the crucified Redeemer shall say to those on his left hand: "Depart, ye cursed, into everlasting fire, prepared for the devil and his angels." This last vision of Christ, and the soul, separated from God, turns away from the throne, and sinks into the depths of that fathomless outer darkness from whence there is no escape, no return, no deliverance. To be separate from God is to lose all the bliss and glory of heaven; it is to experience the misery of the lost in hell.

O that the Divine Spirit might impress upon every soul still separated from God, whose eyes shall rest upon this page, that this is a day of hope. The Heavenly Father calls his wandering children home. Will you come? Will you all come? Will you come now? The time is very short in which life's great work can be done. So much of probation has already run to waste, that the greatest diligence and care must be employed, or death will find you so far removed from God that hope and mercy can never reach you. Every moment's delay in sin thickens the cloud which now but partially obscures the face of God. Every new refusal to accept the offers of divine love builds up a thicker wall of separation between your souls and God. Every new transgression, every cherished sin, increases the distance between the sinner and the Saviour.

O sinner! O precious soul, bought with the blood of Jesus Christ! You are building up an impassable barrier, which will shut you out of heaven. Your sins, if they are persisted in, will drive you to that world of joyless sorrow and hopeless despair, from whence the ear of the omnipresent God cannot hear your cry for mercy, and from whence the arm of the omnipotent Jehovah cannot save you.

# THE DECAY OF WILL.

BY REV. S. E. HERRICK.

I will arise and go to my Father.—*Luke* xv. 18.

This word "I will" was the definite starting-point of a new life. The young man's promptitude saved him.

Into some courses of prosperity men come without any conscious effort of the will to do so. Men are sometimes borne upon the current of circumstances towards wealth and honor. Some are born to greatness, and some have it thrust upon them. Paupers have been known to inherit splendid fortunes. But the new life of a Christian man has its beginning in a single determinative movement.

In saying this, I do not ignore what Christ has said about the "drawing" of the Father. I do not ignore the fact that heavenly influences are secretly brought to bear, and that there may be a preparation of the way with which the man himself has had nothing to do. But, so far as he is concerned, there is an initial

"I will." There is a movement of sharp decision which cuts off, at once and forever, the past from the future. There is the turning of a new leaf, the making of a sharp corner in the life course. The act is as definite as that by which a merchant sets his hand to the paper which terminates a long-standing partnership and begins a new one.

That which gives man all his manliness, and that which makes it possible for him to be like God, is the power to say, "I will." It has been defined as "the power of self-cohesion, or the power to resist changes which take place outside of us." I borrow from the late Dr. Sears an illustration which makes this clear. "If you take a ball of snow and toss it into the stream, you will witness a rapid disintegration of the mass. It grows less and less, till it assimilates to the surrounding substance and disappears. But if you take a piece of quartz and throw that into the water, you observe that it sinks down to the sandy bottom and lies there. The waves beat over it year after year, and it loses no whit of its integrity, but remains an insoluble element in the waves. So let one man be plunged into the current of human society, and you will see by and by that society draws out of him all that was positive and absorbs it. The stream washes out of him all his individuality. His opinions, tastes, sentiments, prejudices, loves and hates, are assimilated and merged in the common mass. Put another person into this same human current and he never is merged in it, but preserves the same flinty outlines amid all the surgings of the waves. He is himself through all changes, and never disintegrated by the current. And the reason is not to be found in intellect, culture, or sensibility, nor in any amount of personal acquirements or accomplishments, but in the amount of will which the man possesses." But the will is something more than the power of self-cohesion, even as man is something more than a lump of granite. It is something more than power to *resist* changes outside of it — it is power to *make* changes. The man of will not only withstands the disintegrating and assimilating forces which play around him, but actually modifies them; not only preserves his own selfhood, but impresses himself upon what is about him. He changes circumstances and makes new ones, even as if the granite could not only retain its own integrity, but change the quality of the waters around it.

Now, whatever robs a man of this power degrades him towards brutishness. It makes him less a man and more a *thing*. What is the most pitiable feature of the drunkard's case? Not his poverty, and rags, and beggary; not his companionship, like that of the very swine — though these things are pitiable enough. It is not at all in the external wretchedness which he has created about him in his home. But it is in his own utter powerlessness to assert himself. He cannot say, "I will." His resolutions perish even before their birth. He may long, nay, there are times when he does long, in the depths of his heart, to rise up against the force of habit and inclination and the moral and social bondage which he has imposed upon himself, and cast them off; but it is as impossible for him as it would be to scale the skies. And there is no sadder sight in all the world than that of a man so enfeebled in this department of his nature that it has not power to bring resolution to the birth; but as often as the purpose is inwardly suggested, its nascent life is choked out by the giants of habit and of circumstance. There is no salvation for him, because the will-power within him is dead. For take notice, my friends, this is the salvable point in a man. This is the point at which salvation lays hold upon him. How constantly Christ appeals to it in his miracles of healing. "*Wilt* thou be made whole?" he asks. "*Wilt thou?*" And he tests this will-power before he heals, by commanding what seems like an impossibility: "Stretch forth that dead hand!" "Rise, thou bedridden cripple; take up thy bed and walk!" And physicians do the same thing now. They know that if they secure the co-operation of a strong will they have an alliance which makes their medicines doubly efficacious. The cure begins when the "I will" is asserted. There is no question, I suppose, that the life of the late Mr. Vanderbilt was protracted, beyond all expectation, by this inward forcefulness of his volitional nature.  So, too, men with a purpose that seemed defiant of danger have passed unharmed through airs reeking with pestilence, have endured what to others of less will-power would have been intolerable and fatal.  So, to use a frequent illustration: "Dr. Kane, an invalid who traveled for his health up in the ice-regions, with the thermometer at seventy degrees below zero, kept off the cold from the seat of life, while stronger men than he yielded to its death-grasp."

It is a wonder that this young man in the parable had not lost the power to say, "I will arise."  For when a man abuses himself as he had done, this faculty is among the first to be weakened.  This power, so regal among the powers of human nature, is sensitive and fugacious.  It subsides and shrinks and vanishes away under abuse or neglect.  It refuses to hold a dishonored scepter.  Its kingdom "is not in word, but in power."  It may die, and its death be unsuspected.  We are told, again and again, how hazardous a thing it is for a young man to enter upon an evil course, with the intention of desisting from it by and by.  Not so much that there may be no by and by for him, but because, when the set time has come, the will may be utterly powerless to assert itself.  The suicide goes on, while neither the man himself nor any one else is aware of it.  What a thrill of horror would come over us if, as we were walking along the peaceful street, some higher intelligence should point out to us one house after another and whisper to us, There, and there, and there, a fellow-mortal is lying in the struggle of death. A more fearful disclosure than that might be made, if we could look into these houses of human flesh and blood. There, and there, and there, a godlike will lies dying. The best that is in the man is perishing. For this power dies while yet the physical strength is firm. This power dies while yet the tender affections of love and friendship flourish. This power dies while yet the fires of intellect and wit are brightly glowing. The house is all bright with gayety and good cheer, and the merry guests come and go; but in its inmost chamber lies the master, dead beyond the power of resurrection.

It is a wonder, I say, that this young man had left enough inward force to resist the inertia that was settling upon him. It is a wonder that he did not think about it and languidly put it off. It is a wonder that having come to the inward conviction and risen up, he did not weakly sit down again among his swine, thinking that it would be better or easier to carry out the resolve on the morrow; and so, like the freezing man who knows not that he is freezing, sink into a deeper and more irresistible torpidity.

And when a man awakes to the fact that the will-power is gone, what a terrible awakening must it be! I have read of one, with a soft and yielding nature, though mentally well-endowed, who had not allowed this inward monarch to summon his powers to their proper subjection and exercise, until by habitually taking away its scepter, he had driven it entirely from its throne. In his age he became reduced to poverty, and felt compelled to write for his daily food. "In order to earn a crust of bread," said he, "I have sat down on a summer's morning, intending to write a story for the magazines; and I have folded the paper, and dipped the pen, and held it in my fingers till it dried; and I have dipped it again, hoping that the thought would come, and gone on in this way till the sun went down, without even marking the paper. Then I grew so weak that I could not come up these stairs, except on my hands and feet, and by and by I could not come at all; and for the last three weeks I have not left my bed, and now they tell me I am dying." Dying, because his will had lost the power to summon his faculties to their proper exercise. My friends, it is a fearful thing to be self-deprived of the power to say "I will"—to be unable to set the face in any right direction and command the feet to go. It is easy to see, too, how along this line of a gradually weakening will, somewhere, there comes the point at which to arouse one's self becomes an impossibility, and so the man is unsalvable. Would it not be wise for us here to-day to test ourselves on this all-important question? Some of us have never said, "I will arise, and go to my Father," under the impression that we could do it at any time—when there shall have come some more convenient opportunity, when the cares of life shall press less urgently, when the work of securing a competency shall be finished, or perchance when somewhat more of life's lower pleasures shall be exhausted. We have been under the impression that the work of salvation is so simple and so easy that it can be accomplished at any time. It is simple and easy only to a mighty will. Are we sure that we can say even now that potent "I will?" Summon yourself to it, and see if your will is still regnant, or whether it do not sink back, exhausted and powerless in the effort.

I know of a man in this city, to-day, of brilliant intellect, one who has been engaged for years in literary work, and who is desirous, earnestly and sincerely so, of taking the prodigal's resolution; but he cannot! He has thorough theoretical knowledge of religion, the highest appreciation of the character and work of Christ, and the tenderest sensibilities withal; can hardly speak of the Redeemer but with tears, and yet, so complete is the paralysis of the will in the man, that for him to become a Christian seems an impossibility. One thing has stood in the way for years, and to that one thing his will has so often been forced to succumb, that it has no longer the power to assert itself. A royal palace, gloriously furnished, but the monarch lying defunct, and his revolted subjects rioting through the halls — a living man, with a dead will. What emphasis and illustration do such facts as this give to those passages of the Word of God which indicate a limitation to the possibilities of salvation. "To-day, if ye will hear his voice, harden not your hearts." "Seek ye the Lord while he may be found. Call ye upon him while he is near." "Now is the accepted time; behold, now is the day of salvation."

But I apprehend that one of the greatest difficulties with men is, not only that the will is weakened and paralyzed, but that they do not know precisely what is the thing that they must have the will to do. The will may be strong as Samson, and yet, like him, blind. There is a conventional way of treating all men who have any desire to enter upon the Christian life, which often does violence to their sincerity, and conveys a false impression. We tell them to "believe in the Lord Jesus Christ." We adopt an answer which was given to a certain man, under very peculiar circumstances, in a very peculiar state of mind, under the pressure of peculiar difficulties, and apply it anywhere and everywhere, no matter whether the case be parallel or not. To be sure, we must all "believe in the Lord Jesus Christ." "There is none other name under heaven given among men whereby we must be saved." And yet many a one could honestly reply, "I do believe in him; I know he died for me; I accept all that you say about the chastisement of our peace laid upon him, and our healing by his stripes, and yet I cannot say that I am a Christian." No, you are not. There is nothing in all this analogous to this determination of the prodigal. What, then, is the precise direction in which this will-power must work? Let us see.

"I will arise and go to my father." Now, take notice, my friends, that this was the hardest thing in the world that this young man could have proposed to himself. It involved the greatest sacrifice that it was in his power to make. It was humiliating; it was mortifying. It crossed his pride; it took down his conceit. Had he not said that he preferred to go on his own way and be the master of his own destiny, and carve out his own life-path? And the elder brother at home, would he not scorn him? And the servants, would they not make sport of him? His resolution, then, amounted to just this: that he would break through the pride which separated him from a return to a true filial life; that he would renounce it, cast it behind his back and take the cross of humiliation, whatever the cost of feeling that it might involve. He knew perfectly well, before he came to this point, that his father still loved him. He knew that the father would receive him graciously; but he did not come into the feeling of a child — he was not a true child — until he said "I will," and assumed the cross which the resolution involved. Then — then — he was a child. Now, some analogous act of renunciation or sacrifice, I believe, invariably stands at the very beginning of the Christian life. When a young man came to Jesus, asking, "Good Master, what must I do to inherit eternal life?" the answer was not, "Believe in me as a Saviour;" but "Go sell that thou hast and give to the poor; take up thy cross and follow me" — giving his will that distinct and clearly-defined obstacle to overcome. That closely-hugged wealth was the thing that kept him from being a Christian. And his will was not equal to the effort. When the publicans came to John, asking the same question, "Master, what shall we do?" he answered them in the same way: "Exact no more than that which is appointed you;" the very hardest thing for a farmer of taxes to do: to give up the only hope of obtaining wealth; to sacrifice even the prospects which the Roman laws allowed him. And wherever in the Gospels the question is asked, you will find that the answer is not given indiscriminately, "Believe;" but the most careful discrimination is manifest in pointing out the cross at the very outset. And it is always a real cross — something that stands in the way of a trustful and filial life; something for the personal will to grapple with. And you will see that the answer which was made to the jailer was given for the same reason. For the proud Roman to give in his allegiance to a Jew—a Nazarene—a *malefactor*—a CRUCIFIED one—what Roman spirit could bear the humiliation? But how he bowed to it. Nay, rather how he rose to it, with a will royal as a Roman's, yet submissive as a Christian's should be!

Now, my friends, for some of you to say "I will arise," would be to go home to your families, and say to them, "I am going to live the life of a Christian from henceforth, so help me God." It would be a hard thing to do, the hardest sacrifice you ever made. It would be such a test of your will-power as it has never endured. For some, it would be to rise and say to your friends in the prayer-meeting to-night, "I ought to be a Christian; I feel the obligation pressing upon me to lead a different life; I will arise; I wish you to pray for God's grace to help me." For some of you it would be, to-morrow morning, to go to Mr. Jones, or Mr. Robinson, and say, "My friend, I have received this money from you unjustly, and I want to restore it. I have been all wrong, and I want to be a different man." Or, it would be to go to your neighbor, whom you have offended, or whom you have injured, and own the wrong, and ask his forgiveness. For some it will be a prompt and decisive surrender of a habit which is breaking you down in body and in soul, and which you cannot keep, you know you cannot, and be God's child. For some it may be the giving up of some long and deeply-cherished plan, which you secretly know is not pleasing to the Heavenly Father, something which is dear to you as life itself. It will make your heart bleed to give it up, but the way of life lies over its ruins.

Then, my friends, "believing in the Lord Jesus Christ" will mean something; it will mean following and being like him, which are a very essential part of being saved by him. But, whatever it be, let there be at once a break — a decisive severing of the past from the future. Let there be no more of this hazardous trifling with the most awful faculty which God has given you. If your will is paralyzed, strengthen the things which remain that are ready to die. Give it henceforth the power that God has put upon it, and of which you have been robbing it. Never say *no* to it again when it turns towards God and heaven. And, with most unquestioning confidence in God's fatherly affection, and in your Elder Brother's atoning love, say, "I will arise and go to my Father." They will come forth to meet you, even from afar. You shall be invested in clean robes, your transgressions forgiven, and your sins covered, and know what you never have known before, an experience of that Father's favor, which outweighs a life-time of all earth's lesser joys, and atones for its greatest sacrifice.

# COMING TO ONE'S SELF.

### BY ANDREW P. PEABODY, D. D.

When he came to himself, he said, . . . I will arise and go to my Father. — *Luke* xv. 17, 18.

It cannot be denied that there is in many quarters of our New England society a degree of indifference to religion, never before so openly manifested, — an indifference in many cases exaggerated into repugnancy, and in many more to be discriminated from absolute unbelief, only in that the questions underlying the faith of the Christian ages are ignored, as not claiming even the show of argument, or the courtesy of consideration. Were all our churches closed, our Bibles destroyed, our Sundays secularized, there are not a few who would be glad, and many would be not sorry. Of our (so-called) Protestant population, the number of intelligent non-church-goers is very large.

Nor is it barely the outward forms of Christianity that are neglected. Its records are no longer an essential part of home education and of daily reading, and, though they retain their place in the Sunday-school, they are studied much less efficiently than was the habit of earlier times, and there are not a few of the now rising generation that know little about them, and care less. Meanwhile, because the literature of the oldest nation in existence—the most influential factor in the world's history—is bound up in the same volume with the Christian Scriptures, it is passing out of the knowledge of educated men and women; though, were the same magnificent lyrics, the same sketches of character, the same morsels of biography and history, in any book but the Bible, scholars would be willing to learn a new language in order to read them.

I have no fear for the ultimate future of Christianity. Because I believe it divine, I have no doubt that it will prevail and triumph. Yet more, the very indifference and preterition of which I have spoken, rightly interpreted, bear testimony to its divinity; if it were not more than human and earthly, it would have, in an age like ours, no dearth of receptive minds. Nor do I think that the world, or our portion of it, is growing worse; but the improvement which is going on now is, in great part, due to influences of Christianity in its more intense and vivid realization, which have not yet spent their force, nor will have spent it before their fountain shall resume its full flow. Of the reforms, social, political, and moral, which have among their foremost advocates men and women who look at the church with no friendly regard, there is not one which was not distinctively Christian in its origin and initial impulse; and society is advancing with a momentum derived from the Gospel it ignores, as a railway train continues to move on an even grade when the steam is shut off. My only concern is for the many who, in their individual characters, motives, and aims, lack the power — at once hallowing, intenerating, and energizing — which goes forth from Christ, and from him alone; and especially for those who are coming forward into life, without even the recognition of truths and hopes which — if only held in unappropriating belief and reverence — would be resorted to in after days, under the pressure of growing trusts, responsibilities, trials, and temptations.

But religion is not alone in the declining interest with which it is regarded. Introspective inquiry, in every department, has lost its hold on the general mind. Physiology has tenfold the attention, curiosity, and research, that are bestowed on the mental and moral constitution of man; the body far transcends the soul in the scale of relative importance; and scores are profoundly interested in the physical parentage of our race, to one who concerns himself about the source, nature, destiny, or even existence, of the spiritual nature. Equally indifferent is the general mind to the principles that underlie the conduct of life. Questions of expediency have the precedence of questions of right; and the right is oftener urged on the ground of expediency, than on that of its own legitimate sovereignty. Indeed, when the highest Christian morality is ostensibly made the rule of life, it is frequently associated with the meanest motives, and Christ is glorified as dispensing the loaves and fishes, rather than as giving and being the bread from heaven.

My text defines and accounts for the phenomena of which I have spoken. The prodigal came to himself before he thought of returning to his father. Self-communion alone can bring us to the Father and to Christ, through whom alone we come to the Father. There is in our time no peculiar indifference or repugnancy to religion as such, or to Christ in his own person; but the habits now prevalent are averse from self-communion. This is due in great part, no doubt, to the immense progress in material knowledge, art and science, in which more than the work of centuries has been crowded within the lifetime of a single generation. The world has so multiplied and intensified its claims upon man's cognitive, apprehensive and active powers, that he lacks breathing intervals for distinct self-consciousness, or can secure them only by forcibly expelling or holding at arm's length obtrusive worldly objects and interests. There will be, in due process of time, an order in this tumultuous chaos; an organization of the conquests over nature; a settled possession and usufruct of the enlarged realm of earthly being; and then there may be, there doubtless will be, a return from over-intense material activity to introspective habits of thought and feeling. But, meanwhile, the needs of the individual soul are all that they were a generation ago, or will be a century hence.

The prevalent aims, made intenser than ever before by the material tendencies of the age, concern, not the quality of being, but its earthly destiny alone. The questions which those indifferent to religion ask themselves are not, What am I? and, What ought I to be? but rather, What shall I do? Where shall I be? What place shall I aim for? What havings shall I seek? On what list of competitors for havings shall I inscribe my name? Many there are, indeed, who do not ask even these questions; but live, as the coarse phrase is, from hand to mouth, with no settled plan or fixed purpose, watching for such opportunities as may occur for gain or for pleasure, and content if they get their dividend of havings from day to day.

Now, a religion that would meet the aspirations of minds of either of these classes would be no religion at all; much less one that was heaven-born and God-given. The first word of a divine religion must rouse men to the consciousness of their individual being, and of the paramount importance of what they are in soul and spirit. He whose utmost desire is satisfied by success in an earthly career — even though that career be the noblest of all, the possession of knowledge and of the power to utilize it — feels none of the wants which religion satisfies, and may therefore be content to ignore it. It is only when he comes to himself, that his career fails to meet his desires and to respond to his endeavors. Let us now consider the new views of life implied in the awakening of self-consciousness.

If I come to myself, what do I need? I need, first of all, my own respect. It is not enough for me that I have the esteem of those around me; that I occupy my position in life blamelessly; that I am growing in consideration, in honor, in substantial success. There are multitudes around me of whom all this is true, yet who have no qualities that command my reverence, no independent traits of moral and spiritual manhood which would make me regard them as enviable for what they are, though they may be so for what they have or for the places they fill. What I want, if I deem my selfhood of any worth, is such an inward character as in another person I should admire and reverence; such a character as, could its environments be made transparent, would win loving regard and deference, even in the humblest position and with the most abject surroundings. Now, I see the elements of such a character nowhere but in the teachings of

Christ; its perfect exemplar nowhere but in his life; its truly venerable representations nowhere but in those who have modeled their lives on his. If I look within, I cannot but compare my character with his, and make him in his perfect humanity my criterion and my judge. Far enough below him I shall, indeed, find myself; but so far as I see in myself any Christlikeness — especially if it be growing in me — I can look on my own inward being with self-complacency and hope. Not so, however, if I find that my virtues are mere prudential conformities; that my habits, however good, have no substratum of inward principle; that I am a mere factor, however important, in the mechanism of society, and not a self-conscious integer in the commonwealth of souls. Thus I cannot come to myself without resorting for my self-respect to him whom he that has seen with the vision of an appropriating faith has seen the Father.

But it is not enough that I take on the traits, or even breathe the spirit of Christ. I cannot respect myself, unless I am assured of my Father's complacent regard; unless I hold a child's place with reference to him. Here, whatever my present aims and aspirations may be, I encounter the memory of sins that have merited his displeasure, and I cannot but recognize a law of the lower nature still in conflict with my better self, — with the law which the inner man has chosen. I need forgiveness, and the assurance of it.

I do not deserve it. I cannot promise it to myself. I know not where to look for it, but to Christ and his Cross,— to "God in Christ, reconciling the world unto himself, not imputing their trespasses unto them." It is in the suffering Saviour that the Father comes forth to meet his penitent child, to throw around him the arms of an undying love, and to extend to him the welcome home which else the sinless alone might have claimed.

But not only do I need his forgiveness for the sins, which I repent and forsake. As his being is the most essential fact in my being, so is his constant approval my most constant need; his favor, my true life. I have his love, his yearning love, let me be what I may. The yearning of that love can be satisfied, only as I am always his,— as I look to him for daily guidance, commend myself ever to his blessing, live always as in his sight, and make my work worship, my enjoyment praise. To acknowledge the being of God in seasons of devotion, and yet to ignore it in any part of my daily life, is as absurd as it is impious, and if I care anything about my own selfhood, I cannot tolerate in myself intervals of practical atheism, even though they alternate with religious hours; but I shall employ the most strenuous self-discipline, and shall earnestly implore the aid of the Divine Spirit, that I may walk ever as on holy ground, and live ever as within temple gates.

Yet more, if I come to myself, I must needs have an aim and a career, for my self, for my soul, for that which is the seat of principle, affection, and character; and what is that aim, that career, what can it be, other than growth in goodness, the perfecting of character, progress in devotion, love, charity, in all the graces of the Christian spirit and life? This is the only career which is not self-limited, the only aim which I can pursue while life lasts. Let me enter on the most desirable earthly career that can open before my ambition, if my days upon earth be not prematurely cut off, before, probably long before they terminate, I shall have reached my ultimate goal; I shall have exhausted the possibilities of my position; I shall have passed the climax of my enjoyment of whatever it can give me; I shall see myself, if not displaced, surpassed by younger rivals; and the best that I can hope is a quiet, and not unhonored, decline, and a close gracefully rounded off. More probably, the decline will be reluctant, with the painful feeling of being thrust aside, and with retrospective longings for what has gone from me irrevocably. Such a career, indeed, I must have, as a citizen of this world, and if I live long enough, I must step aside from it before I die. All the more, therefore, do I need a career on which the lapse of years will not arrest me, — which I may pursue even the more vigorously when heavier burdens are laid on my patience and my cheerful trust. The growth of character need not be reverted, or suspended, or retarded, by any earthly vicissitude. It ripens in the late autumn. It mellows under the frosts of the declining life-year. When the steps become feeble, and the memory treacherous, and the active powers the mere shadow of what they were, the love of God and man, submission and resignation, faith and trust, may still be on the ascendant; and the years, when there shall be no longer the capacity for pursuits that begin and end on earth, may find the soul still advancing on the heavenward career, its evening shadows glowing in the morning twilight of the unending day. Thus may be verified the words of the prophet,—when, as to things earthly, on the once fruitful vine there shall be left only "two or three berries on the top of the uppermost bough, four or five in the outmost branches,—at that day shall a man look to his Maker, and his eyes shall have respect to the Holy One of Israel."

But it is not age alone that arrests the earthly career. It is at the mercy of misfortune, human caprice, change of opinion, unnumbered casualties. How many there are who, by no folly, mistake or fault of their own, falter and fail early or midway! Nay, how many who find no room for so much as an entrance on what they would fain make their lifepath! Many more than would be imagined by one who had not had a lengthened period of observation, lead lives of perpetual disappointment; never begin to realize their aims; never find their places, and see only the reverse side of their hopes and expectations.

We all, then, equally need a lifelong career,—an aim which we can pursue with no possibility of failure; and this we can have, only if our aim be the noblest of all,—that of moral perfectness; our career the highest of all,—that of the love of God, and the pursuit of that which has praise and honor with him.

But we need more than a career that shall close only with death. We cannot believe our life earthbounded. There is an instinctive longing for immortality. The man who comes to himself is conscious of the capacity of an endless being, and he goes to his Father as to the Author and Giver of the life eternal. With the memorials of mortality constantly before and around us, we ought to take death, nay, early, speedy death, into our plan of life, and to make our career one which death shall not suspend. The only aim with which we ought to be satisfied is one which can be pursued alike on either side of the separating stream. In the near view of death I know that there is not one of us who would be contented with aught short of a character that shall find its congenial home in the society of heaven. This and this alone can smooth the declivity that slopes graveward; this alone can loose the pain of dying, and make the approaching close of the earthly life serene and happy.

Two or three weeks ago the principal of one of our great scientific institutions described to me the condition of two of his assistants, both consciously death-bound. One, he said, was a man of large attainments and of a high order of ability; but, in his illness, was alternating between welcome seasons of prolonged lethargy and awakenings of bewildering solicitude and racking apprehension, in which the future seemed to him utterly obscure and hopeless. The other was an unlettered porter, who had led a life of simple, earnest piety, and who was waiting in daily expectation of death, with unfaltering hope, and notwithstanding frequent attacks of intense bodily agony, supremely happy in the clear and realizing view of an open heaven. The one had a career which fatal illness had closed forever. The other had an eternal career, in which death could make no break. Be our attainments what they may, our culture no matter how large and high, when the last earthly home approaches we shall need to find ourselves on a career on which we can say, "Death, I am not thine, nor canst thou arrest me on the way which I have chosen. Thou canst but speed my progress on that path of the just on which thy shadow casts no gloom, while the Lord God sheds upon it eternal light and everlasting joy."

I cannot close more fittingly than by quoting Luther's expression of the contrast between the earth-bounded and the eternal life-career.

The formula for him who lives for earth alone, is:

> "I live, but, ah! how long,
>   I do not, cannot know;
> I die, but know not when,
>   Nor whither I shall go.
> Why, then, I ask with wonder, why
> Do I thus live in ease and joy?"

On the other hand, the soul in which the eternal life has begun on earth sings:

> "I live, and I can tell
>   How long my life will last;
> I die, and know full well
>   When Jordan will be passed;
> How I shall die, and whither go,
> The Lord hath made me clearly know.
> Why, then, I ask with wonder, why
> In sadness should I droop and die?"

H

## THE CRY FOR A CLEANSED HEART.

**BY REV. ALBERT E. DUNNING.**

---

Create in me a clean heart, O God; and renew a right spirit within me. Cast me not away from thy presence, and take not thy holy spirit from me. Restore unto me the joy of thy salvation; and uphold me with thy free spirit. Then will I teach transgressors thy ways; and sinners shall be converted unto thee.—*Psalm* li. 10-13.

IN our noblest moments only two objects are before the mind: God, and one's self. These are the moments that give sweetness, and harmony, and power, to our lives. No one who does not often, and deliberately, with a profound sense of need, pray to God, "Create in me a clean heart," can pray with any hope of answer, "Restore unto me the joy of thy salvation, and sustain me with a free spirit." There is no such joy except to the clean heart. There are no clean hearts except those which God has cleansed, in answer to the cry of need. The spirit of adoption, willing and generous, is a pure spirit.

In this time of religious interest, many say, "I am not moved. I know I ought to be a Christian, but I have no feeling." Thousands in this city to-day are waiting for feeling, and when that comes they expect to be saved. This is their excuse for sin. They try to cast the responsibility for their uncleansed hearts on God. What step must they take in order to realize the divine presence? A holy choice makes you realize the touch of the holy God. Feeling can no more continue without action, than music without sound. How can you feel deeply, unless you welcome feeling? When God touches the keys of your soul, you must give forth sound. When one truthfully says, "I want, most of all, a clean heart," he puts himself into an attitude to see God. "The pure in heart *shall* see God."

One cloudless midday I saw groups of men and women in the streets, gazing into the sky. I looked, and could see nothing. I could not understand it. It seemed as if some mad folly had seized them. I asked an explanation. "We are looking at a star," said one. "It shines so brightly that you can see it at midday." He guided my eyes to a point where two telegraph wires crossed each other. Instantly, the white dot was visible in the blue. Men were exclaiming on every side, "Oh, I see it plain enough!" It seemed strange that I had not seen it before. Yet, as soon as I changed my position and looked up, the sky was blank again. You can see and feel God only along the line of a holy choice. That alone will bring over you the awe of the Unseen Presence.

The experience of the unconverted, and of the Christian who has lapsed from God, are similar here. We lose sight of him if we do not seek daily cleansing, and daily renew our vows. Often the beauty and grandeur of holiness have won from us admiration, and a degree of self-denial, without bringing inward peace. But as soon as our souls are set with a supreme purpose to do his will, his overshadowing presence fills, and profoundly moves, the soul.

Men say, "We don't believe in revivals, they are attended by so much excitement." But if *one* man sets himself to be pure in heart, and repents of his sins, the new sense of the presence of God will make a profound impression in him, and on his friends. If thousands of Christians turn anew, one by one, with the sincere prayer, "Create in me a clean heart," it will occasion some excitement in them. You cannot help it. Would you rather have them refrain from the excitement, than have them clean? If thousands, who have never offered that prayer, begin to pray, it makes a good deal of excitement, and some mistakes may be made. But what shall we say of the helpfulness, and what of the hearts of those whose only interest in the prayers of multitudes for clean hearts is their fear of the excitement, or their amusement at it?

Now, when our resolve to be holy is made, our helplessness is made manifest. We cannot make pure our impure selves. Then the cleansing blood of Christ becomes inexpressibly precious, and we welcome the joy of his salvation. You have heard of it a thousand times. But all at once you feel your personal, absolute need of it, and appropriate the wondrous gift. Is it strange that men are excited, and shout for joy as they receive it? Heaven rings with such excitement — the hallelujahs of the redeemed. Those who cannot welcome such excitement, and are disturbed because the city is so full of it, are preparing to be still less able to bear it, and to say to the mountains and rocks, "Fall on us, and hide us from his face."

You cannot escape from God. You may fly from the joy of his salvation, from the expressions of cleansed hearts: but no region is so remote, no shelter so thick, as to hide you from him who is "of purer eyes than to behold evil." It has been well said that the only way to fly from God is to fly to him. Let me mention, then, three kinds of obstacles that come between us and God when we go to him to ask for cleansed hearts.

I. *Our own sins.* We must give up all purpose to sin before we can come to God to be made clean. Many think that God is going to change their wills by some sort of mesmeric power. There is no ground for such a hope. If you prefer the satisfaction of an unforgiving spirit, or any sinful habit, you can have it. But you must choose between that and a cleansed heart. You cannot have both. You are to change your will, and put self into the hands of a holy God, and he changes your heart because you want it changed.

This choice extends to everything we possess: position, property, affections, ambitions. There is dishonesty in every possession that we hold in our own names. It is kept by the basest of frauds, and makes a clean heart impossible. Not long since I saw an advertisement on my neighbor's house, "For sale." I was surprised. He had recently built it, with the hope of spending his life in that home. I called on him. He told me he had become bankrupt. He had surrendered house, shop, store, everything, to his creditors, and they had let him the house, and had employed him on wages in his own shop and store. Just so we are bankrupt. We owe to God a great debt, far more than we can ever pay. The only honest course for us is to surrender everything into his hands, and become stewards of what he entrusts to us.

You know how desperate men get when conscience troubles them, and they refuse to give up certain darling sins. They go to God and lie, in prayer. They say, "Create in me a clean heart," when they will not have it made clean. I have known men who frankly declared they would not forgive others, and therefore did not use the prayer our Lord has taught us to use.

I have known them to pray with seeming intensity of earnestness to be pure and holy, lying unto God. I know men who frankly acknowledge that they know God commands them to surrender themselves to him, to accept Christ as their Saviour and Lord, and they will not do it. Yet they keep up the habit of prayer. They come to God just as if they meant to do his will, and pray: and they do not mean to do his will. They think God does not know it, or overlooks it, or excuses it. What other evidence do we need that the heart is deceitful and desperately wicked?

Sometimes people say it is cruel to tell the unconverted that God will not hear their prayers; that many moral men do not accept Christ's cleansing, but they have religious sentiments, and God is a being of love, and will not turn any away. But when any one, converted or unconverted, comes to God in prayer, God always put to him this question, "Will you obey my will? Will you give yourself up to me?" He puts that question in his Word. He puts it in the conscience. If one says "No" to that question, it is foolish, and wicked, and desperate self-deception, that leads him to make believe he is praying. "The thoughts of the wicked are an abomination to the Lord." His sins are right between him and God, and it is his business to put them out of the way. "Behold, the Lord's hand is not shortened, that it cannot save; neither his ear heavy, that it cannot hear; but your iniquities have separated between you and your God, and your sins have hid his face from you, that he will not hear. \* \* \* Your lips have spoken lies."

But let one once resolve to put away his sins, and with a sense of his own unworthiness flee to God to be cleansed, and all heaven rings with welcome. The Spirit says, "Come." The bride says, "Come." They that hear say, "Come." Heaven thrills with joy over one repentant soul. Let a man begin to be honest with himself, and honest with God, and all who love holiness are glad.

But we make a terrible mistake when we seek to quiet conscience in any other way than by coming to God to be cleansed from sin. There are hours when we care little about God; when goodness does not win, and evil does not startle. But there are other hours when we want to be holy; when we realize that an uncleansed heart is mean and vile in the eyes of all the universe. What we feel to be true in our best moments, remains true in all moments. We ought to tremble if cleanness of heart has ceased to be an object of concern. Men say "there is no penalty for sin," when the penalty has already fallen on them. Is a frozen thermometer an indication that the cold has ceased?

A little child was lately found sleeping beside a lady, and neither had wakened at the morning call. But because both were equally silent, was there no woe in that house? The child, when touched, moved, and quietly opened her eyes to the light. The lady answered not, moved not. She had died without a sound. A pure conscience responds to the touch of God, like the sleeping child to the touch of her friend. A deadened conscience is like the lady who had died without a sound. There is no other but the restless, tossing conscience, "like the troubled sea when it cannot rest, whose waters cast up mire and dirt." But can we offer a deadened conscience as a substitute for a cleansed heart, when we come to stand before God in judgment?

There is a terrible reason for the skepticism of those who have fallen away from God. "I cannot believe as I used to," men say. How can one who means to carry an uncleansed heart believe in heaven? He has no interest in it, for "there shall in no wise enter into it anything that defileth." "Holding faith, and *a good conscience*, which, some having put away, concerning faith have made shipwreck." When once the good conscience is put away, faith is shipwrecked. How can a moral nature, riddled by sins, hold faith? Faith leaks out of him like water out of a tub that has been baked in the sun. There is no genuine faith without a heart that is cleansed from sin. If we would cry to God for cleansed hearts, we must first renounce our sins.

H*

II. *The imperfections of those who wish to help us, stand between us and God.* You start to go to God and pray, "Create in me a clean heart," and you turn to look at the imperfections of one who is trying to lead you there. There is a standard of esthetic taste, of physical beauty, of literary culture, of devoutness of manner. Men stop short of God because the means he has provided to guide them to him do not come up to their ideal.

At the Centennial Exposition, a mechanic standing before a picture was overheard speaking rapturously in its praise. "Isn't it splendid? I did that." "You did it?" said an astonished bystander. "Why, this picture is by an eminent French artist, and here is his name in the corner." "Sho," was the reply, "I mean the frame."

Just so when by human lips "Christ hath been evidently set forth, crucified among you," we talk of the man, his manner, his language, his surroundings, the effect on the audience, but not of God manifest in the face of Jesus Christ, looking forth from this frame. Here is where the peculiar difficulties of cultured Boston lie. Men have talked of frames, the way they fit the picture, their color, the spots on them, and think they have displayed a fine taste. They talk much of books written about God, of theories about God, and have been proud of the display of culture. We have talked little of the Holy Being whom we need to cleanse our hearts, because that involves self-abasement. We have been critics of frames, and have boasted of it. Oh, if you will look earnestly at the picture, you will find a healing balm for bruised, soiled hearts, and the frame will fade from sight. Our habits of criticism are a cankerous vice in society, eating out the heart of truth. We have picked out the bones and left the meat, till God has sent us leanness of soul. The husks of criticism are swine's food. Christians stand in the way of thousands coming to God to be cleansed by calling attention away from the picture to the frame. We ask too often, "How do you like Moody?" and too seldom, "How much do you love Jesus Christ?" God never meant that his ministers should be perfect. "We have this treasure in earthen vessels, that the excellency of the power may be of God and not of us." The vessel that God honors let us honor, and get treasure from it.

We spend too much time discussing the different methods of Christian work, while our hearts are uncleansed. It is like giving a keynote in music. One takes a note from one, another from another. All try their voices by each other: and then, when we undertake to sound the same chord, what a discord there is! But let each one go alone to the organ, and take his keynote; then when we come together, there is harmony. Oh, friends, let us not be getting our soul-music from each other. Let each go with his own sinful heart to God, and offer this prayer of the text. Then there will be harmony in our opinions and work.

III. *The sins of others are in the way of our coming to God.* Here I must be brief. This is a common excuse. "My neighbor professes to be a Christian, and he has many faults. Therefore I am going to keep my own heart vile and uncleansed, because I judge him to be a hypocrite."

> "He cannot smell a rose, but pricks his nose
> Against the thorn, and rails against the rose."

Away with such folly! Is he to judge you, that you can retort on him at the judgment?

The best of us are turned aside by stumbling blocks; and the Word of God is terribly severe on those who make even one of the feeblest to offend. But if we stumble over others, the fall will not hurt us less because they were in the way. The cry of each one, who knows his own heart at all, is "How can *I* be clean?"

An uncleansed heart is a vile thing.

Each one must go alone, and meet God alone, with the prayer of the text on his lips, if he would be cleansed.

Infinite love has provided for our cleansing. I will not offer you the words of man, at this solemn moment, when the cry goes forth, "Create in me a clean heart." But there rises before us a figure of One not of earth; he holds forth in his hand a red symbol; and, behold, it is blood, and he speaks as he holds it, "This is my blood of the New Testament, shed for many for the remission of sins."

God might justly cast us from his presence. What a glorious thing that we can be cleansed!

A clean heart that is a cleansed heart, and there is no other, is powerful to convert men.

Many say, "I never could talk with others about their salvation; I am not qualified." I know it. I do not ask you to do it. But each can get his own heart cleansed. This precious truth is for you. You can put aside every sin, shut out all the imperfections, all the sins of others, and come penitently before God to be cleansed. You can renew that prayer hourly. It is your privilege; for we hourly need the answer.

I will not urge one who has done, and is doing this, to work for others; to expose his imperfections to others' criticism. Once let the Spirit fill the heart that is emptied of self, and it will find and occupy the place to which God calls it.

Create in me a clean heart, O God!

# GOD'S CONTROVERSY WITH HIS PEOPLE.

### BY ALEXANDER H. VINTON, D. D.

---

The Lord hath a controversy with his people. — *Micah* vi. 3.

THE prophet Micah, proclaiming the Messiah, prepares his way to the hearts and minds of Israel by a solemn reproof: "Hear ye now what the Lord saith. Arise, contend thou before the mountains, and let the hills hear thy voice. Hear ye, O mountains, the Lord's controversy, and ye strong foundations of the earth; for the Lord hath a controversy with his people and he will plead with Israel."

Startling, indeed, is the summons when the Almighty comes out in his distinct personality, and calls upon man as a moral agent to stand up and answer his complaint. Impressive, indeed, is the transaction in which Jehovah lays aside his sovereignty for the while, and meets his creature face to face and tells him to justify or condemn himself out of his own mouth. And solemn, too, is the scene where the universe attends that trial, and even the inanimate things are endowed with hearing and a mind, as assessors in that judgment. Even the dull earth listens, and the mountains and the hills, from summit to summit, shall echo the verdict round the world. Alas! for that Christless soul who shall be cast in that lawsuit. That witnessing earth still listens—those creatures of God still live.

The Almighty has known no change. The judgment still waits. The Lord has still a controversy with his people. The millennium is not yet. I would bring this thought down to our time, and to this congregation, that there is an issue pending between God and your souls, on which hinges nothing less than divine sovereignty and human salvation. It is by no means the pleasantest part of a minister's duty to tell his people so. Sweeter far are the emotions with which he stands up and proclaims in the assembly the message of mercy; to tell how that mercy waits to bless; to show that Mount Calvary overtops the heaped-up guilt of men, and that the blood-stains of the Cross are not yet covered and obscured by their clouds of sins. But it sometimes happens that when mercy is a familiar thought it grows to seem too easy, seeming only *mere* mercy, and willful sinners and careless Christians lap their souls upon it and go to sleep. And then it becomes necessary to mention in the people's ears that grace has conditions, that grace supposes a controversy, and to tell what that controversy is. It is plain enough at first sight that it is a controversy in which the advantage is very unequally divided. It is a controversy between power and weakness, between wisdom and folly; a controversy between authority on the one hand and willfulness on the other; and finally, since God is good, it must be a controversy between right and wrong.

This view of the question makes our case eminently bad. But it shows, at least, the amazing importance of the quarrel. Whatever be the subjects of difference between God and men, nothing can be more full of solemn moment than the difference itself. And let me add that although the advantage seems thus all on one side, this controversy was not of God's seeking.

It is often the case, that conscious power and security beget a superciliousness which is the most stinging provocative to a quarrel. Modesty and weakness are sometimes stirred up to virtuous rebellion against the superiority which is grown too arrogant to be borne. But this controversy was not so provoked. God did not make man to quarrel with him, but to bless him in his body and soul; to nurse him with the joys of heaven; to exercise him for the life of heaven, and to lead him there — and man would not. This is the true position of the question. And yet let me add, in the third place, that although it was not sought nor invented by our great God, this controversy is *mutual*.

There are complaints and charges on either side, which must be abandoned by one party or the other before they can come together in peace. There is no room for compromise. There are no equal interests to claim a mutual concession by both parties. They meet in open contradiction. The one party, full of love, and wisdom, and parental tenderness, had prescribed the way of peace and prosperity to man, and then said, Do this, and thou shalt live. The other party, no less full of impatience and self-will, replied, "I will not do it, if I die." To justify his impatience, man brings accusations against God. To vindicate his goodness, God replies to these complaints, and so a formal issue is made, and this is the quarrel which is to be arbitrated before the universe, if it be not sooner tried at the bar of each man's conscience, and adjusted at the mercy-seat. And what are these grounds of accusation? How do we men undertake to criminate the Most High? Do not start at the expression, nor refuse it, until you have entered into your own hearts and read the meaning of your most secret thoughts of God.

What are those common complaints, uttered or unuttered by man, according as he is bold or timid, which form the matter of this great controversy. My brethren, I might say that these complaints go to the whole extent of God's relations to this world. They embrace all the varied manifestations of the divine character. Never did heaven come near the earth, but the earth found fault with it; or God speak to man, but man found something in the matter, or the manner, to criticise, something that was either unreasonable or in bad taste. As we cannot specify all the divine manifestations, we classify them into these—the divine law, divine providence, and the divine grace of the Gospel. Let that man, who has never quarreled with each and all of these, stand up and avouch his guiltlessness, and God will answer him, God will crown him or convince him.

First—The first great subject of controversy is the divine law. Men quarrel with its letter and with its spirit. Men dispute its specifications and its generalizations. Its specifications are in the Decalogue, beginning "Thou shalt have no other God besides me," and ending with "Thou shalt not covet." And what article of the Decalogue has been unresisted by what man? Its generalizations are in that revised law which embodies the whole life of religion, "Thou shalt love the Lord thy God, with all thy heart, and with all thy soul, and with all thy mind. This is the first and great commandment. And the second is like unto it, Thou shalt love thy neighbor as thyself." And who of us all can lay his hand on his heart, and say, That law is in me, a part of my nature, written on my heart. I love it like my life. My best and happiest life is to obey it. Look around, and mark, and learn, my brethren. Here is a man of business, and full of business. He has a passion that rules him, absorbs him, night and day, namely, to be rich, not to support his family merely, not to serve God with his wealth chiefly; but to support his family in more expensive luxury, and to serve God and charity, subordinately and incidentally. He means not to neglect either, but one thing he means above all others, to be rich, if he can, and for the sake of being rich. And this is idolatry as much as if he should carve out his ruling passion in solid gold, and call it Mammon, and burn incense before it. He does burn incense to it. For, from his heart, which is an altar,—for every human heart is an altar, which sends up its tribute to some god or other, hot and reeking with the fumes of its strongest loves,—from his covetous heart rises an incense of desire and devotion, whose unspoken meaning is, " Gold, thou art blessed, bless me with thy gifts." He could not say more to the God of gods. He does not say so much.

Look around you again. Here is the politician, seeking not fame, not that surviving fame which outlives nations, built on moral heroism, despising the clamor of present praise, for the sake of eternal right and truth, but seeking simply office, the mere badge which fame sometimes wears. For this badge, this gewgaw to draw wondering eyes, what does he sacrifice? Time, truth, moral consistency, and all genuineness of character; yea, he makes a whole burnt offering of himself and his sacred being to the demon of party, the profanest of unholy worship. To be called Rabbi! See him when he is grown old and great, yet never great enough. He must advance from one Rabbi's seat to another, and if he cannot, the cankering ambition eats into his soul's pith, and makes it the mere blasted shell of a soul. His consumed life has been given to an object which is not God, but a god. Look around you again. Here is another living creature, living for the excitement of what is called pleasure. It may be the pleasure of fashionable society, idle pleasure, or the deeper excitements of passion, gaming, licentiousness, intemperance. Harmless as some of these pleasures are, and bad and unholy the others, yet they are allied in their principle. They all make pleasure the aim of life, killing time and indulging self, and hence they are apt to be found together in one circle of society, borrowing countenance from each other, and all of them sanctioned by omnipotent fashion. And so omnipotent fashion is a god. Not to be more specific, take any or all of these examples, and though not a single votary of wealth, ambition, or pleasure may openly complain of God's law, yet what say their lives? Are not their lives a living daily protest against that law? Tell them what Jesus said, "Thou shalt love the Lord thy God, with all thy heart, and with all thy soul, and with all thy mind," and if the man of business do not content himself with a shrug of contempt at your simplicity in bringing religion on 'Change, and if the politician do not quietly sneer at your holding up the honors of heaven against the solid emoluments of office, and complain that you join church and state together, and if the young man and woman of fashion do not wonder at your illiberality, and turn away and chase some new fashion; if they should treat the subject soberly, and answer out of their hearts, they would say, "Oh, it is too hard to love God and Christ better than all these. It is unnatural." So they quarrel with the first and great commandment of the Law.

Take the second commandment, "Love thy neighbor as thyself." To know whether we quarrel with it, see how we act.

To learn how far a man regards his neighbor's interest, trade with him; or his neighbor's convenience, travel with him; or his neighbor's feelings, let him be raised a little above him in fashion and popularity; or his neighbor's life, see him in a shipwreck; or a neighbor's reputation, be present when that neighbor is absent and witness the ingenious dissection which brings out his seeming faults and pares down his good qualities, or underlays them with bad motives. See how a tale of scandal, or only a suspicion of one's virtue, floats in at men's ears and out at their mouths, till it seems to be the very atmosphere of the city. We know it would not be so, if we were all loving brothers and sisters together. And not behaving like brothers and sisters, we quarrel with the great law of God and Christ in our hearts and lives. And now what is the answer of God in heaven to these common complaints of men? for here lies the controversy. "You are my creatures and I your sovereign. I had and still have a right to you, body and soul. If I make a law, you ought to obey it." He might stop here and we should be dumb. But he adds, "That law is the type and form of my own character — the character of the loveliest and best; you quarrel with an eternal excellency." He goes on: "That law is the rule and method of perfect peace. If it were universally obeyed, would not earth be Paradise again? It is likewise the way of immortal life — was meant to guide you to glory. You refuse your salvation. I cannot bear to see you die, and so I plead with you in controversy against your own wrong. Plead with me," he says: "Let us reason together." "Give ear, O ye mountains, and let the hills hear thy voice." And while this part of the controversy stands recorded for trial, let us pass to the next complaint of man towards God, for he no more acquiesces in divine providence than he assents to the divine law, — the providence of God, that tangled web in which we can trace no steady lines of purpose, but only chance and confusion. Looking upon it at large, man sees nothing but arbitrary will and inequality: here all light, and that the brightest, and there all gloom of melancholy depth.

One nation is civilized, another cannibalized; and for no apparent reason. One race is progressive in all ennobling attainments; another hopelessly unteachable. And in a nearer view, the complexity is worse. Health, wealth, talent, power, are the born attributes of this, — and wretchedness, with all the wants which perpetuate it, the heritage of that man; and this is the ground of complaint. The poor pine, because the rich revel. The rich rebel, because wealth cannot buy health and domestic peace. The widow murmurs, because God hath taken away the right arm that supported her. The father, because his son, in whom he expected to live over again, is gone first. The man who has lost his fortune and cannot begin to toil up the hill of enterprise again, sorrows with many a surging feeling of angered pride; and vanity, disappointed, is turned from a mere weakness into a sour passion, because its beauty has faded, or its talents been slighted, or its great friends have cast it off. Almost as various as the facts of history are our complaints of Divine Providence. Scarcely anything satisfies us.

Listen to the wise plea of the all-wise Disposer of things: "Thou murmurest at my dispensations. Dost thou not know that I smite and wound in order to heal? and if sorrow comes twice or thrice, it is because you would heal your own wounds falsely, and I tear them open to heal them from the bottom? If I snatched away the gay wife, was it not to save the mourning widow? If I snatched away the jewel son, was it not to endow the father with the manliest virtue—submission to *his* Father—and save him from idolatry? If I made you poor, was it not because prosperity is not a means of grace, and it is hard for the rich man to be poor in spirit enough to gain the kingdom of heaven? If I spoiled your beauty, or put a bar in the way of your talents, and defeated your social ambition or your political, remember it was that you might find a friend who was more than an admirer, and 'an honor that cometh from above.'" Let your conscience weigh this divine argument, my brethren, for it will be weighed in the balances of the sanctuary, when the Lord's controversy is settled for eternity.

And now, once more, and finally, God's creatures quarrel with his grace and Gospel, and this is the spirit and meaning of their complaint: "Are the virtuous no better than the vile, that they must both be saved by one method, and that method humiliation? Does it require atoning blood to wash clean the souls of high and low alike? Will not my honorable dealing, and my reverence for religion, save me from stooping down to that low level where the wretched congregate when they ask for salvation? Are we both to be saved by mercy, neither of us by merit? Do we, whose lives are so correct, need new hearts?"

Such is the plausible criticism of refined circles

against the abasing doctrines of the Saviour God. They contest them at every point. They refuse the Cross and the Crucified, and they complain not loud, but deep. And God answers them from on high, "I have done all I can. Heaven and earth bear witness. I can no more. Sinners by birth and practice both, when you had broken my law, and had no escape from doom, I made my Gospel, gave my Son, sent my Spirit, have waited, am waiting, and because in my kind providence I have saved you from the accidents of poverty and temptation, you think yourselves too good and high to accept my dearest gift— that gift which exhausted my power to save." Each of your objections betrays its origin in hateful pride. There is no way to save you but by humiliation, and humbled you will not be.

I know not how this divine argument affects you, but it seems to me to shut every mouth, and place the offending soul where it will stand at last, shorn of excuse. This obedient universe may well be summoned to attest the righteousness of the Most High; but, oh, when the trial comes, there will be a felt witness in the sinner's own hopeless soul that equity and justice are the habitation of God's seat. The issue is made up. The trial only waits for the signal. We none of us know when that signal shall strike. But this we are assured of, that if any man carries this controversy to his death-bed, his last pulse beats the knell of hope to him forever. But, thanks to infinite grace, the last pulse has not beat yet. The signal of judgment has not struck, but only the Sabbath summons of mercy. "Though your sins be as scarlet, they shall be as white as snow; though they be red like crimson, they shall be as wool." Happy the soul that has become reconciled through the Cross, that walks in the light of God, and by daily divine communion and holiness attests that the controversy abides no more, but only the beauty and blessedness of friendship with God.

# GOD A CONSUMING FIRE.

### BY REV. A. J. GORDON.

*For our God is a consuming fire.* — *Heb.* xii. 20.

By a very natural antithesis we have become accustomed to set this definition of Jehovah, "Our God is a consuming fire," over against that other one, "God is love," as indicating the two opposite poles of the divine nature. But perhaps the definitions are rather identical than antithetical. The same fire that burns and consumes, also warms and illuminates. The same love that comforts and caresses, also chastens and afflicts. What if we say then that God is love — a love which burns and chastens us when we abuse it; and which gladdens and blesses us when we obey it? We shall then avoid the misconception into which we so constantly fall, that God's punishments are the result of his justice alone, while his mercies are the issue of his love. There are distinct and different attributes indeed in the character of God. But it may be that these are all resolvable into the one underlying and primary attribute of *love,* even as the colors of the rainbow, when blended, resolve themselves back into the original and colorless white. At all events, we have constantly in the Scriptures the illustration of attributes issuing in their opposites. "Whom the Lord loveth, he chasteneth"—love punishing. "He is faithful and just to forgive us our sins"—justice pardoning. And so we learn that we have no right to imagine that God has ceased from his love because he afflicts us, or that he has ceased from his justice because he forgives us. He is one, and indivisible in his actions, as he is one in his being. He does what he does, with the consent of all his nature; and the most opposite and irreconcilable manifestations of his providence, as they seem to us, all harmonize no doubt with him in the unisons of perfect love. The musician, with the full melody in his mind, touches now a very soft and limpid note, and now a very stern and rugged one, in bringing out that melody. And so it is in the oratorio of Divine Providence. As the spirit rehearses it by the mouth of David we hear such strains as these: "To him that smote Egypt in their first born—*for his mercy endureth forever.* To him which smote great kings—*for his mercy endureth forever.* And slew famous kings—*for his mercy endureth forever.*" And strange and almost incongruous as the refrain may seem to us, we are sure there can be no inharmony.

Seeking now our interpretation of the text directly from the Scriptures, we have these lessons:

I. The inapproachable holiness of God.

Jehovah first revealed himself to Moses in the burning bush — "the bush that burned with fire, and was not consumed." And as his servant turned aside to see this great sight, the Lord called unto him out of the midst of the bush, and said, "Draw not nigh hither, put off thy shoes from off thy feet, for the place whereon thou standest is holy ground." Had Moses come nigh, we may believe that he would have been consumed, as Nadab and Abihu were, for their sacrilege, when "there went out fire from the Lord and devoured them." This seems to be the lesson. The holiness of God, self-originated and self-sustained, glows on forever like a fire. It is unconsumed itself, for there is nothing in it that can be destroyed. But the unholy man would kindle and waste before it like the stubble, were he to approach it.

And in saying this, I do not utter a merely mystical and inexplicable saying. In the sphere of morals, purity is just as scorching and caustic in its action upon impurity, as a flame is upon fuel. The sanctity of a truly consecrated man is an annoynace to his unconsecrated neighbor; and to his godless and impure neighbor a positive torment, if he is compelled for any time to endure it. There is more than mere contrariety between sin and righteousness, there is an antagonism which tends to mutual repulsion or extermination. If water is thrown upon fire, either the fire will be put out or the water will be vaporized, according to the relative strength of the elements. And if sin comes in contact with holiness, it will either quench that holiness or be itself consumed and overpowered by it. And it is in this sense, I believe, that it is true that the holiness of God is a consuming fire. Not that there is any heat of vindictive anger in it; not that it is surcharged, like the thunder-cloud, with the elements of destruction, ready at any moment to leap forth and smite the wicked. But that it is so intrinsically and eternally opposed to sin, that it must scorch and wither that sin when it is brought in contact with it.

And I am sure that this is a most important lesson for us to learn. The sin of the age is irreverence. There is little putting off of the shoes of worldliness and unspirituality, in coming into the presence of the Most High. With what light familiarity, with what flippant and presumptuous freedom, we approach the King of purities. The doctrine of the infinite paternity of God beguiles many into a most unfilial liberty; and they who are by nature "the children of wrath" hesitate not to climb upon the knee of their Heavenly Father before they have been washed or sanctified by his Spirit, and to touch with unclean hands his feet which are "like unto fine brass, as if they burned in a furnace." We cannot dwell too much upon the believer's privilege to say, "Abba Father;" but neither can we remember too carefully or fearfully that only he that hath clean hands and a pure heart can ascend unto the hill of the Lord or stand in his holy place. Behold the priest about to enter within the curtain of the tabernacle. First he must come to the altar, where lies the sacrificial victim; then to the laver, wherein is the water for making clean the hands. Only thus atoned for and washed could he enter within the holy place and look upon the bright and burning cherubim. And were these types only meaningless symbols, think you — the shadows of facts and requirements that have ceased now that grace has superseded law? Nay! holiness and the requirements of holiness are alike unchangeable from age to age. Look up to the true Tabernacle — the Holy of Holies — in the heavens; and then listen to the solemn words of the Apocalypse: "And before the throne was there a sea of glass like unto crystal." The laver of the heavenly tabernacle is there, — the brazen sea of the upper temple, telling by glowing symbol what is elsewhere declared in literal and solemn language, that "there shall in no wise enter into that place anything that defileth, neither whatsoever worketh abomination or maketh a lie." And we are defiled by sin and therefore must be cast out, unless we have been justified by the blood of Christ and sanctified by the washing of regeneration.

Our heaven, let us never forget, depends on *what* we are, and not on *where* we are. And I fully believe that we cannot imagine a greater punishment for an unholy and reprobate soul than to summon it into the unveiled presence of God. To have the Eternal Eye forever upon him — that eye of holiness which is joy and life to all holy things — would be to him a flaming fire of punishment. There need be no anger in that eye; only the beaming vision of eternal purity. There need be no flashes of divine displeasure in it; only the dazzling whiteness of the great holy soul shining calmly and forever forth. And yet this gaze would be intolerable to the sinner. It is in the very nature of things that it should be so. The calm, benignant face of Purity is as terrible as a tropic sun to the naked sinner. "Oh, whither shall I go from thy spirit? or whither shall I flee from thy presence?" is his cry. Even the rapt and holy Isaiah, as he saw the Lord sitting on a throne high and lifted, cried "Woe is me, for I am undone; because I am a man of unclean lips and dwell in the midst of a people of unclean lips: for mine eyes have seen the King, the Lord of Hosts." It is the pain of infinite contrast. As the gleaming flash of lightning throws into strong and startling relief the objects which the night had covered; as the sudden entrance of the sunlight shows that the air which had before seemed pure now is mixed and turbid with the motes that float in it, so will the soul of the darkened sinner be astonished and dismayed as by one glance of his burning eyes, the Lord shall set his iniquities before him and his secret sins in the light of his countenance. "Blessed are the pure in heart, for they shall see God." The purity which they share in common with him who is the source and centre of all pureness will be as a pellucid atmosphere, revealing to them the light of his countenance, and yet tempering and assuaging the naked fierceness of that light, that it may not smite them. But the impure, with no such protecting or revealing medium, will be dazzled and struck to earth by the sight. The beatific vision of the pure will be to them a vision of terror. Oh! friends, how can we stand before God unless we have Christ for a shield and covering? The sight of his burning face is enough to overwhelm us. How significant that saying concerning the doom of Antichrist. No fiery darts are shot at him from the battlements of heaven. No flaming sword of vengeance is drawn against him. The Lord simply shows himself to him in his glory. "Whom he shall destroy with the brightness of his coming."

II. We may infer from these words the unsparing righteousness of God in making atonement for sin.

Recall that scene in the tabernacle. Moses and

Aaron had come forth and blessed the people, and the glory of the Lord had appeared to them. And then the record proceeds, "there came a fire out from before the Lord, and consumed upon the altar the burnt offering and the fat; which, when the people saw, they shouted and fell on their faces." As the altar sacrifice is a type of the great atonement, is not this event the foreshadowing of what happened to the Lamb of God? Literally was he, the spotless victim, consumed for our transgressions, as the burning penalty of a broken law came forth upon him from the Father. God is always God, and sin is always sin. And as certainly as the fire must scorch the fuel with which it comes in contact, so certainly must the righteous judgment of God kindle upon iniquity whenever it is found. Therefore when "he, who knew no sin, was made sin for us," the burnings of divine penalty fell upon him, till he was consumed upon the altar and yielded up the ghost. "God spared not his own son." Nay, though with strong crying and tears, he pleaded that he might be spared, and though with deathly faintness and bloody sweat he shrunk back from the impending blow, yet God spared him not. Spared him not, that he might spare us. As the rays of the lurid sun, passing through the burning glass, leave the glass untouched and unaffected, but burn and scorch the object in which they find a focus, so — think of it, oh, ye that esteem sin a little thing — the burnings of God's penalty against sin were not restrained or softened in the least, but they passed through a race of sinners, leaving them unscathed, and, lighting on him, the sinless one, who was the focal man of our humanity, consumed him unto death for us. I know not why it need be said that the wrath of God fell on Jesus Christ. Perhaps we should speak as truly if we said that it was only the kindlings of his righteous love that smote him. I ask you to bring together two sentences from the Bible, and tell me if such depths in the mystery of love were ever touched before. "This is my beloved Son, in whom I am well pleased." "Yet it pleased the Lord to bruise him." Here is no anger. Here is no burning of vengeance or indignation. It is love, but a love so righteous, and so just, that it is pleased to smite, and smites the one in whom it is alone and supremely pleased. It is a great mystery.

Now we see again at this point how squarely this doctrine goes against the current sentiment of the day respecting God. It is just the belief that God is not a consuming fire that holds a multitude of minds in easy irreligion and good-natured self-complacency to-day. There may be some fire in his judgments, it is admitted. But it is held in check by his gentleness. It is restrained by his loving kindness; it can never kindle upon a sinner to his hurt. It cannot be a consuming fire, for the sparsest shower of tears can put it out. But I ask you to look not into the world of the lost, but to the Cross of Christ, and learn how terribly God punishes sin, and how consuming his judgments are against transgression. In our estimate the guilt of sin is lessened according to the degree of purity of the character in which it is found. We are inclined to punish leniently the offense of him whose life has been generally correct. But when sin was found upon the sinless Son of God, the penalty fell just as heavily on him as though he had been the guiltiest of the race. God, who in the beginning declared that he would "by no means clear the guilty," cleared not his Son when the iniquity of us all had been laid upon him, but freely delivered him up for us all. When he had made the soul of his beloved an offering for sin, it became as true as in the tabernacle. "There came a fire out from before the Lord, and consumed the offering upon the altar."

I dwell upon this fact not to impress you with the severity of God, but to make you see the inviolable justness of his love. From the Cross we hear God saying, "I have loved thee with an everlasting love." And if, looking up, we ask, "Who art thou, Lord?" the answer comes, "I that speak in righteousness, mighty to save." "When were love's arms ever stretched so wide as on the Cross?" and the roots of the Cross are embedded in the deep foundations of eternal justice. God punishes that he may forgive. He burns the sacrifice to ashes on the holy altar, that the law, at length satisfied, satiated, if I may say so, by the offering of the spotless Lamb, may speak pardon to him who has broken it. And thus God is severely just, that he may be the justifier of him that believeth.

III. The words of my text teach the retributive justice of God against the finally incorrigible.

"For the Lord thy God is a consuming fire, even a jealous God," are the solemn words with which Moses concludes his warning to the children of Israel against apostacy. "The Lord was angry with me for your sakes," he said to them, "and forbade me from entering into the promised land." "Take heed to yourself, lest ye forget the covenant of the Lord your God." And well may we take warning. If God spared not his beloved Moses, how can he spare us, if we continue in disobedience? "If the righteous are scarcely saved, where shall the sinner and the ungodly appear?" The Lord has a holy jealousy against sin, that, however restrained for the time, must at last go forth in consuming terror upon evil-doers.

We have no lurid delineation of hell to set before you, but this much is certain: the fire must sooner or later kindle upon all wrong-doing. Happy are we if we bring our sins to that altar where the Son of God, on whom our iniquities are laid, has become our burnt offering, that we might be spared from the eternal burning. And even here I dwell not upon the anger of God against the wicked. How do we know but his wrath, as we call it, is but his love kindled to its white heat? Fire burns not fire. And if we have the love of the Father in us, kindling into ever-growing ardor and intensity till he comes, when he reveals himself from heaven, in flaming fire, we shall not be burned. The fire that shall fall upon an unbelieving world with overwhelming terror, will only cause his saints to shine like the firmament forever and ever.

Let me now, in closing, draw just the lesson from my subject which is found in connection with the text: "Let us have grace whereby we may serve God acceptably with *reverence* and *godly fear*, for our God is a consuming fire."

Do you reverence God, my hearer? I do not mean by your bearing and postures in the house of God. I do not mean by your devout propriety and religiousness in your treatment of Christian subjects and ceremonies. These are the mere accidentals of reverence, signifying very little of themselves. But do you reverence him so much that you shrink from coming into his presence with unrepented and unforgiven sins upon you? That is the most searching test. Moses dared not draw nigh to the flaming Jehovah. But with an effrontery which is as characteristic of men's religion as of their manners in this age, there are those who, without a scruple and with no shield or panoply of faith, would rush into that presence where angels fear to tread. Sin is no hindrance; lack of faith is no hindrance. Want of spiritual acquaintance is no hindrance. Nothing is more appalling than this familiarity of vaunting unbelief. I tell you, if you have nothing upon you but the sandals of a self-righteous and fleshly boldness, you had best put off your shoes from your feet, and stand afar off, and come not nigh until you have had "your feet shod with the preparation of the gospel of peace."

Do you fear God, my hearer? I do not mean, do you sometimes tremble before his coming judgment? Do you share that fearful looking for of the indignation that shall devour the adversaries? That is but the fear of a slave, the terror of a servant. But do you fear him so that you are afraid to sin before him? or that, having sinned, instead of hiding from his presence you are impelled to come before him and confess your guilt, that he may cleanse and justify you? If not, you know nothing of "godly fear." The fear of God is one thing; godly fear is quite another. The one is the dismay of terror: the other is the filial caution of love. The one trembles for the safety of self: the other is solicitous for the honor of Jehovah. The one cries out, "Oh, I am afraid of God; whither can I flee to escape his sight?" the other says in those grand, sweet words of St. Augustine, "I am afraid of God, therefore I will run to his arms."

"Our God is a consuming fire." What do those words mean to you, my hearer? That you, having been tried like gold in the furnace of his discipline, shall be found unto praise and honor and glory at his appearing? Or that you shall be only like the chaff, burned and utterly destroyed by contact with a holy love rejected, with a Saviour disbelieved, with a spirit grieved and rejected?

# GOD DISMISSED.

**BY SAMUEL L. CALDWELL, D. D.**

---

Therefore they say unto God, Depart from us; for we desire not the knowledge of thy ways. —*Job* xxi. 14.

THERE is some awful centrifugal tendency in the human heart carrying it away from God. It finds language here. It is the wish put into the lips of prosperous wickedness. Wealth, pleasure, success, all earthly blessing there may be, and yet with them dislike, forgetfulness of God, — even on account of them. *Therefore*, says Job, they say unto God, Depart. The connection between great worldly prosperity and spiritual ignorance, and utter godlessness, is not unaccountable, is indeed quite natural. They do not necessarily go together. But, with much or little, this ancient poet spoke out the feeling of many a man, a natural, a common, I may say a universal, feeling of the human heart. There is much desire, seeking after God, if haply it may find him. Let us not deny that. There is much joy over the knowledge of him and his ways. Souls there are, in churches, in multitudes, to whom the vision, the knowledge of God, is the great joy of existence. Let us never depreciate the actual amount of religion, the belief in a living God, the power of Christianity, which prevails in spite of every bad influence, against great, perhaps growing, ungodliness. But neither let it be forgotten that there is another side. That we must look at. We must listen to the voices all around which are saying, Depart; no God for us. What is the Almighty, that we should serve him? and what profit should we have if we pray unto him? This is the effort—it manifests itself in many ways—to put God as far off as possible, out of thought, knowledge, faith, desire, existence even. This is the spirit of many a man's life, of much social custom, even of literature, of science. It is God, a personal, living, true, present God, men dislike, exclude. I am not anxious to make out a bad case against anybody, to represent people as worse than they are. Let everybody have credit for as much religion as he has. But after that, it is still true that, consciously or unconsciously, there is the attempt to separate and exclude God, to put him off and away; if not utterly, then as far as possible.

I do not undertake to say how far the attempt to exclude God from nature springs from moral causes; but it is very noticeable that there is this scientific tendency. It is the effort to construct a theory of the universe in which a God is unnecessary. It is the effort to discover a natural origin for all the forms of life; to trace them to spontaneous generation rather than divine will; to endless processes of evolution rather than to the creation of God. There are scientific hypotheses which hold a God in reserve, a superfluous Deity, who is pushed back into a remote distance, where the language which the Hebrew Psalms, which Christian feeling applies to him, is absurd. Of course, God is not a subject for science, which deals with phenomena. God is not at the end of the telescope, or the microscope. No analysis, no dissection, no experiment, pushed however far, discloses God. He is a spirit, not to be apprehended by science, but by faith. Science is not to blame that it is not religion; that it confines itself to the facts of the universe, their origin and relations—if it only did confine itself to that. But suppose that through science, through whatever theory, by whatever method, a man succeeds in exiling God from the world, separating nature from a living and almighty Creator, turning nature into a God, knowing no other than the force which manifests itself in all life—so making religion impossible; so saying to the Almighty, Depart from us, we desire not the knowledge of thy ways,—he is doing a dreadful wrong to his soul. He is sacrificing the knowledge of God to the knowledge of his works. And that there is this unbelieving, atheistic tendency, this removing God farther and farther off, this substitution of nature, its forces, laws, evolutions, processes, results, for God; and that it goes along with scientific inquiry, with the better knowledge of the ways of God in nature, which it calls nature's own ways, is evident enough. Faith, knowing there is a God, comes to nature, desiring a knowledge of his ways; and rejoices to follow them as, dark or shining, they go through infinite space. It follows his paths in the elder world, when life was first moving in the mists of creation's morning. It follows them in the orbits of stars and galaxies, beyond the borders of the day. His footsteps are in the deep waters, and on the mountain tops, and there it finds them, fossil or fresh, alike the track of a living God. But unbelief, having no desire for him, goes after science, into every corner and privacy of the universe, to find it occupied with all signs of intelligence, of will, of power, but no God.

Is there no similar tendency in regard to the Bible, to Christ; no disposition to exclude God from that which to faith is a revelation from him? For here is this great fact of Christianity in the world. Here is a Book full of God. Here is Jesus of Nazareth, full of God. And what is to be done? One course is to push it all as far away as possible, to keep it out of sight, out of thought, in the realm of fiction; to exclude it with God himself. Another is to push God out of it, and so reduce its importance, in fact destroy its truth. For if you exclude God from it entirely; if in origin it is purely human; if it is simply a human view of life, a human speculation about the future; if Jesus Christ comes from himself, and not from God; if you can subtract, can expel, all divinity from the Bible, it has no force for the conscience, no authority, no controlling, saving influence over the soul. Either way, this is the difficulty, the objection. It is to God, to God dealing with sin and sinners. Its spirit, its language is, Depart from us; we desire not the knowledge of thy ways. For this the Bible gives— knowledge of God and his ways. This it brings home to the heart, the fact that there is a God with whom we have to do, and that his ways are not as our ways. If you can exclude God from it, silence his voice in it, make it the voice of mere ventriloquists trying to imitate God, then its power, its value, is gone — the terror it is to the bad, the hope it is to the good. And this is the attempt, for whatever reason. In some cases it is because the Bible makes a man uncomfortable on account of conscious unlikeness, opposition to God. It is to relieve the mind from a presence too searching, too pure. It is to escape the trouble which God's commandments make. It is the spirit which, in the old time, said, Depart from us; we desire not the knowledge of thy ways. This the Bible gives. And this sin, unbelief does not want.

God is not only in his works and in his word, but in life, and this spirit would exclude him from that. The Bible, faith, bring God near. He is present everywhere. All things are under his control and his providence. He has to do with men. It is not fortune, but God. He kills and he makes alive. He gives and he takes away. He is dealing with men. He rules. He has not set the world going and left it. He is not a dead God, an absent God. He is not impotent or indifferent. His eyes are in every place. His power is upon all things. Our times are in his hand. And to faith his providence is visible every moment. God is all and in all. Nothing is absent from him. Not a hair falls without him. No change which he has not appointed. But how easy does the spirit of the text find it to remove God out of life— to separate it from his providence? It may recognize a fate, an awful destiny, an unescapable necessity in life, but never God. For a time it may feel a sort of independence, supremacy, that life is what we make it, till some convulsion, some awful reverse, comes. Even then it refuses God, the God of love and truth, the Heavenly Father, any place. It is a dreadful life to live, amidst the uncertainties, the dangers, the losses, at the mercy of so many forces clashing together to destroy our blessings and even ourselves in a moment, and yet no God to care, to help. And yet some prefer this, and say in their hearts, Depart from us, for we desire not the knowledge of thy ways.

And it is not Providence only — a fatherly inspection and direction on the part of God. It is his moral rule. It is his righteous government. It is his holy presence and authority. This men want to put away as far as possible; out of sight at least, out of existence, if they could. It is God in this character, doing what such a character requires; it is God holding us up to accountability, revealing, maintaining, enforcing a moral law; it is God dealing with men on principles of justice, drawing the lines between right and wrong; it is God declaring the law on Sinai, on Calvary, in the high places of the soul; it is God making men know their sins, know his wrath against iniquity; it is God not only revealing but enforcing the law, the God who runs out actions to their consequences, who not only foretells but actually brings retribution; it is the pure God, the punishing God, that men want to flee from, want to depart from them. That story of Adam hiding among the trees of Eden with conscious guilt is the story of the human soul forever fleeing from the pursuing sword of that Holy One who follows it in all its transgression. It cannot bear the light, and shelters itself from God as best it can. It wants to keep God anywhere but in the very life it lives, and in the secrets of an evil heart. Strange it seems that this mysterious soul, coming from God, most like him of anything in the universe, turns its back and flees from him. If it were not for conscious sin it would fly to his embrace and want to know him, to feel his touch, to hear him, and look upon him, and be with him. And, indeed, at last that is the reason why it does go to him and cling to him, when it finds that he can cure it, that its only refuge is there, and that his love is great enough to cover it, and pure enough to cleanse it.

For there is again the grace, the Spirit of God, coming into life; the only hope of life corrupted and lost. For God is equally present with law and love, with retribution and remedy. He is revealed to the conscience as its disturbance and its peace. He smites and heals. His Spirit pursues the human soul not only with dark memories, and terrible accusations, and fearful prophecies, but with promise, and an arresting, delivering hand. To every one of you he has been so revealed. His voice has been heard by your inner ear in many a tender, thoughtful hour, and it has been a voice of love rather than of wrath. It has said, Come; and you have said, Depart. It has said, I love you with everlasting love; and you have responded, I desire not a knowledge of thy ways. God has come near with power to convert your heart, to melt it into penitence, to set it right, to turn it back to him; and you have repelled him, you have gone away from him. I am not using the abstract language which tells what may be. I speak directly to persons who have moral natures; who have some knowledge of God, of themselves; who know enough of their inward life to remember these visits of a Spirit which has flashed the light of another world across their path, and made God a reality for a time, and has compelled you to wrestle with a God who wanted to subdue you that he might help you; whose purpose of love and salvation was in his eye and voice. And against this God you have striven; not against his wrath, but his pity and his mercy. You have had the fearful power to push him back, and close the door, and shut him out. It is not the sword of justice you have fled from alone. It is the good angel. It is to God wanting to help and save you that you have said, Depart; thy way I will not go in; I desire not to know it.

Now, the reason, the philosophy of all this is not hard to find. It lies in one fact, in one central, controlling fact. It is not that God is not worth knowing; or, as the agnostic says, that he cannot be known. It is not that the human mind would not find in him something greater, more satisfying, than in his works. It is not that human souls have not upward aspirations. It is not that thought, that all our nobler powers would not find highest employment in the search after God. It is not that he cannot be found, or that when found he is hard and hateful.

No, the knowledge of God and his ways is condemning. It obliges us to confess ourselves in the wrong. It puts us at moral disadvantage. It creates trouble. Left alone we take our own way, and have no fear. But let the light of God steal into the heart; let him surround the soul, and into its depths go from all sides the condemnations which need no uttered words of his, which spring up in the conscience at the very thought of his presence, at the very sight of his face. It is of no use. You may resort to whatever speculations you will, you cannot ignore this sober, eternal fact of opposition between the sinful soul and God. Your science cannot get over it. There is something in us which is not right, not at peace with God. No matter what you call it, it is there. And as long as it is there, the soul wants to put God away until the blessed moment comes; when, defenses all broken down, it desires to go to him and end the quarrel, and have everlasting peace. But as long as sin rules, as passion and bad inclination and selfishness will have their way, contrary to God's way, so long there is opposition and the thrusting of God out.

This is the awful moral phenomenon which the Bible discloses; which is visible enough to honest observation; which perhaps seems to you only a relic of old-world theology, hardly worth repeating; unworthy, perhaps, of an enlightened and liberal mind. But, my friends, we cannot get round it. I speak honestly, plainly about it. Why should we want to get round it? Why not wish to know the facts of our moral life, of the spiritual world, as of the material? Why not this first? Knowing this thoroughly, we have the key to deeper mysteries than science opens. We see into the mysteries of the human heart, and of God's grace in dealing with it, and are prepared for the faith which not only sees him and believes his Word, but which goes to him and begs him never to depart, but to be our God forever and ever.

The cause of this aversion, repulsion towards God, is moral. That no man can doubt. And if he looks into himself he finds why he is so far from God; why he does not want God any nearer; why, in moments of wrong and conscious sin, he wishes there were no God, and that he could have his own way to the end. But there is the result as well as the cause. What is the consequence of a man's saying this, and continuing to say it?

The first is, that God does depart. I will not pretend to go into the heart of God, and tell what goes on there. I only describe the moral fact. However it happens, whether by God's act or ours, the soul and God go farther apart. He is more and more remote. The fear of him weakens. The vision of him fades. The thought of him contracts. He may be here just as close as ever. But the moral distance constantly widens. He ceases to be felt. Communication stops. He is withdrawn, even from prayer, as behind an impenetrable veil. He cannot be seen. You go where he is, where others find him, even in his house, and he is not there. His Spirit has retreated into the dark and the silence, grieved.

As a further consequence, the soul is left without God. It is left to itself, with all the evil there is in it, the irrepressible inclinations, the insurgent passions, the inflammable tempers; with all the temptation, the danger, the kindling excitements, the terrible pressure of the world. With whatever restraints, it is left without those which come from God, his conscious presence, his wholesome fear. With God so far off, his inspection forgotten, his judgment in the invisible distance, himself but a name, what is there strong enough to hold sin, and keep it under? And to be without God, is to be without hope. There is hope in outward things, as long as they last. But such hope is very brief, very uncertain, very shallow. There is no real hope, solid enough to outlast death, except in God, and in the moral condition of the soul, unalienated, reconciled, living with God here, and going to his society hereafter. You have dismissed him, he has departed, and there is no hope in him left. And without salvation too. For that must come from God, and from God consciously near and welcome. Forgiveness, spiritual health and restoration, cannot spring up in the soul itself. They are not the gift of nature. They do not come from without, or through human channels. It is the touch of God, the life which comes with the presence, the vision, the love of him. Our destruction is in alienation from him. Our only salvation is in return to him, in his return to us, in that double return and actual union, which he has made possible in Christ Jesus.

I do not like to leave off with only this dark picture of a God dismissed, departed, unknown because undesired. It is possible to know God and his ways. And this knowledge is spiritual power, is eternal life, is heavenly glory. It is possible even for God to come back to a soul which has sent him away, which, seeing the terrible condition in which it has been left, rouses itself and goes after him, and finds him at last and forever at the Cross of his Son. It may be that he stands even to-day at the door, and knocks, himself seeking a way back into some alienated heart. At any rate, he has not gone so far away, even from you who have wandered into the darkest distances, that he cannot be found. Look up, you shall see that he is nearer than you think. Open your ears, for you may hear his footsteps. Cry to him, even in your despair, for he can hear a long way off. Forsake everything for him, and you shall find him, and he shall keep you and bless you forever.

# JESUS OF NAZARETH PASSETH BY.

### BY REV. ALEXANDER McKENZIE.

And they told him, that Jesus of Nazareth passeth by. — *Luke* xviii. 37.

A BLIND man at the wayside, by the gate of Jericho, begging: the stir of a multitude arousing his attention: the eager questions, Who are these people? Whither are they going? the answer of some who heard him, "Jesus of Nazareth passeth by:" the anxious cry from out that "nighted life," "Jesus, Son of David, have mercy on me:" rebuked, but the more earnestly repeated, "Son of David, have mercy on me:" the hastening of the man when he was called: the word of divine power and mercy, "Receive thy sight; thy faith hath saved thee:" the breaking in of light upon his long darkness: the gladness with which he glorified God and followed him, — these are the simple, but, out of the gospel, unexampled events which are found in the thrice-told narrative which a few words have now brought to your notice, — "Jesus of Nazareth passeth by."

The important thought in these words is, not that he would soon be gone, but that he was then at hand. Where he had been, or where he would be, was of less consequence. At that time he was passing. The golden moment had come to Bartimeus. He knew his opportunity and filled it with importunity. To the present Christ he cried for mercy; from the present Christ the mercy came. That the time was brief, that this was our Lord's only visit to Jericho, would have been fatal if the man had lost that passing moment, but did not work against him, because he seized his chance with a quick hand and grasped its blessing. We have much to say of the rapid flight of time. We give to the fact an undue importance. That time flies is of little consequence if we are awake and alert. There is time enough for life; and time is slow enough for duty. "To everything there is a season, and a time to every purpose under the heaven." Only we must be prompt, and keep up with duty, and pay as we go; ready to "catch the transient hour;" "improve each moment as it flies." If we "be called upon to face some awful moment to which heaven has joined great issues," we can meet the trust with composure and fulfill it thoroughly. A man can go as fast as the horse he rides; as fast as Time which carries him. Miss this minute, and you may never have another like it. Neglect this duty, and you may never have time to do it. But put each duty into its own place and the duties of life will be done. What is passing has not yet passed. Think where it is rather than where it will be. Time moves rapidly. Events hurry on. The present is soon the past. This onward movement is designed for our advantage. It is like the pressing forward of the ship which bears us home. It is also like the speeding of the ships which bring our treasures to us. Time has brought us to this hour, when here Jesus of Nazareth is passing by. Prophets and kings desired to see his day, and died without the sight. His coming might have been delayed till our earthly course was run. Two days more delay, where a thousand years are as a day, and we had lived and died waiting for him to come, if, indeed, we had heard of him. But time has hastened on with him. He came to Bethlehem and Nazareth; he finished his work; he died for men; he rose again and ascended. We have heard his words: have seen his works: have watched by his cross and sepulchre, and gazed after him as he went up on high. The rapid march of providence and grace has let us see our Lord. Nor is this all of the past. His bodily presence is withdrawn for a time; but he is still here. He came into the world to remain in it till redemption was completed. He is Jesus of Nazareth, not of heaven merely: of this world, of every Nazareth. He is here this morning. This is his house; this is the day of his resurrection. Here are his words with the promise of his presence. We have sung to him; we have prayed to him; upon his mediation have we laid our souls. He is here: for "Where two or three are gathered together in my name, there am I." Some of you have in you the witness of his presence, spirit in spirit. Others, I trust, feel his presence, a drawing towards him, a desire to be blessed of him.

Who is here? Emmanuel, God: God with us. Why was he called *Jesus?* Because "He shall save his people from their sins." Why is he here? To bestow the gift of God upon us. It is peace, rest, light, life. "I give unto them eternal life; and they shall never perish." "I am the Resurrection and the Life." "This is the true God, and eternal life." "Jesus of Nazareth passeth by." Shall I say that to-morrow he may have passed, and be out of sight? It concerns us more to feel that to-day he is here, — passing by, but within our call. No man knows how long that will be true, but he is here now. To-morrow! we may be dead. Before another sunrise our destiny may be sealed forever. Or, living, the impressions of this hour may have left us. The cares of the world may flow in upon us and efface the thought which is born and nurtured in this sacred place. Very fleeting are good impressions and good resolves in this busy world. The disposition to ask for mercy may vanish with the day. To-morrow we may have forgotten the Sabbath. Or, again, the special influences of this time may be withdrawn. It is the Holy Spirit who inclines us to come to Christ. God in his sovereignty calls us, moves upon us, pleads with us. He may not visit us in this way to-morrow. He may leave us to our idols; to our hardened hearts, which know not the day of their visitation. "Then shall they call upon me, but I will not answer; they shall seek me early, but they shall not find me." All this may come to pass with us, as it has with so many others. The old lament may rise, "The harvest is past, the summer is ended, and we are not saved." But why need we talk of what may be to-morrow? We are living now, not then. I tell you a greater truth than these. That Christ should be absent from Jericho was not remarkable. That he should be present there was remarkable. The thought that he may leave us is very solemn. It is of more immediate importance to think that he has not left us. The fact, and the corresponding privilege of this hour, I pray you, have regard to these. Now, here, "Jesus of Nazareth passeth by." Let us fix our minds upon the present and its opportunity. He passeth by. The blessings which he brings are close at hand. If we speak, he hears. If we ask for sight, he gives it. In a gracious conjunction of events, the needy are in the presence of the helper; the sinner is before the Saviour; the guilty are where forgiveness is offered to them.

I. In the presence of this fact you will notice, first, that we have not to wait for God's blessing. Already it is waiting for us. The preparation for being helped is being needy. We are prepared. Now we labor and are heavy laden, and that is preparation for the rest which Christ will give. Now we need guidance and strength and comfort, and that is preparation for the gifts of light, power, consolation. Now we need the new heart, or, having that, the quickened and perfected heart; and that is preparation for the Holy Spirit. We are guilty; and guilt needs pardon and removal, which come only through the Saviour who now is passing by. Our need of Christ can never be more real, can hardly be perceptibly greater, than it is to-day. What shall we do, then, but cry, " Jesus, have mercy on me — on *me?* " But one must feel his sins, it is said; and I have no feeling. He should feel his sins enough to stop sinning. The deeper his sorrow over his past life the better. I think you wrong yourself, my friend, if you say you have no remorse for an ungrateful, disobedient life. What you have to do is now, with whatever emotion you have, to accept the mercy of God and pledge yourself to a life of piety. To wait for feeling is so long to remain in ungodliness. Wait for nothing. Let conscience and reason have their way, and pray, " God be merciful to me, a sinner."

Must I not repent? That is repentance. Turning

from wrong to right, from self to Christ, that is repentance. Feeling will attend the act; but the virtue is in the turning. Must I not have faith? That is faith. The act by which you commit yourself to the mercy of God, in Christ the Saviour, is the act of faith. Must I not have a Christian life? That is a Christian life. It is the beginning of an endless career of trust and service. Must I not be converted? That is conversion: the turning around of the soul and the life, so that you look on Christ, and follow him. Must I not be born again? That is being born again: having the will, the affections, the purpose, the choice of life changed, renewed, brought into agreement with the will of God. Must I not have the Holy Spirit? This is the work of the Holy Spirit, moving you to penitence and faith, making you the child of God. If we will be blessed, God will bless, and now he passeth by where, in our need, we are awaiting the judgment towards which time bears us with relentless speed. A blind man at the wayside. Jesus of Nazareth passing by. The cry, "Son of David, have mercy on me." The gift of sight: the opening of a new life of praise and gladness. This is what we need to reproduce. While the mercy is here, we have not to wait for it. While we need it, we have not to prepare for it. If we will ask it, and receive it, he will bestow it. Now is the accepted time. Should it not be the day of our salvation?

II. You will mark, in this connection, that we have no need to go on in sin. We can be forgiven, and can receive a new principle of life. If at any time we do wrong afterwards, it will be contrary to our ruling purpose — an exception and not the rule. The course of our life will be towards God; and, though the currents may turn us from our course, we shall still be making headway towards the desired haven. The works of the flesh and the fruit of the Spirit are distinct; and if we are under the control of the Spirit of God, we shall do the works which please him. And the character of the life, its motive and intention, will be righteous. Into this life we can enter if we will accept the mercy of Christ, who to-day is here, and the new life with the new motive can begin at once.

III. It will be seen, therefore, that we need run no risk of missing the gift of God. Let the morrow bring what it will, we have made the grace of God our own. We may be in the midst of exciting business, or weighty cares, but they will not take from us the mercy we have received, nor keep us from having it. If sudden death removes us from the world, it cannot undo our choice of life, nor keep us from the Saviour to whom we have given ourselves. The present made secure, the future is our own. We are masters of the position. We protect ourselves from the risk of losing our souls by saving them. The choice is made. The deed is done. Come life, come death, we shall not fail of mercy, for we have received mercy. Calmly, confidently, resting on the certainty of faith, the soul can say, in humility and gratitude, "I know whom I have believed, and am persuaded that he is able to keep that which I have committed unto him."

IV. It is to be remarked, further, that by the right use of this time, when Christ is passing by, we save the rest of life for good uses. If the design of religion were simply to get us from perdition into paradise, it would matter little when we come to Christ, so that we are not overtaken by death before we have received his mercy. Finding from the tables of life insurance companies how long we are likely to live, we could determine how long it would be prudent to live in irreligion — without God, and without hope. Delay would be dangerous, for life is always held by a slight tenure. Youth, strength, apparent health, are often disappointed; and when we look not for it death knocks at our gate, and we are gone. It is not prudent to put off till to-morrow what it is indispensable that we should do. On this matter of the uncertainty of life, we have seen so much we are not in darkness, that that day should overtake us as a thief. "Watch ye, therefore, for ye know not when the Master of the house cometh, at even, or at midnight, or at the cock crowing, or in the morning: Lest coming suddenly, he find you sleeping. And what I say unto you, I say unto all, Watch."

But perilous as it is to put off the time when we will take God's mercy, it were less hazardous if merely to get into heaven were the sole purpose of religion. The design of religion is very much more than this. Rightly to be fitted for a saintly life beyond this world we should have made a holy use of every day from our birth to our translation. Though the years were fourscore, there were not an hour too many to fit us worthily for eternal blessedness. We have shortened the time and increased the work. Every day spent in irreligion gives us more to do and less time for doing anything. We cannot be too quick in laying hold upon the lapsing hours. The son of Timeus should get sight as soon as possible for his own sake. If he has a family dependent upon him, or public duties to discharge, it is more needful that he improve his first opportunity. In regard to our personal piety, each one has himself to think of, and others also. Piety is not another name for selfishness. It is another name for love. First, we ought to think of God. Our life all belongs to him. We cannot give him the whole, alas! But we can give him all that remains, which now is more than it can ever be again. Never again shall we have so much time as we have now for gratitude, affection, obedience. Shall we drain the cup of life on the chance that we can give to God the dregs? Shall we take the feast and leave for God the crumbs which fall from our table? Are youth and manhood for ourselves, and only age, with its deepening shadows, for our Heavenly Father?

> "Oh! Father abbot,
> An old man, broken with the storms of state,
> Is come to lay his weary bones among ye;
> Give him a little earth for charity."

We need all the time which remains, also, for perfecting ourselves. Conversion and regeneration begin a work which is to go on as long as we live. We are to "grow in grace, and in the knowledge of our Lord and Saviour Jesus Christ." To faith are to be added knowledge and charity, and all virtues. St. Paul describes two lives as two houses. Both are on the good foundation. But one is made of wood, hay, and stubble, which must be burned; and the man will be saved alone, and so as by fire. The other is of gold, silver, and precious stones, which will be transferred with the man and be his wealth forever. The longer we live well, the more treasure shall we lay up in heaven. We need all the remaining time, also, for usefulness. There is much we ought to do which we shall not do till we are Christians. Much in our houses, much in society, much for the wide world. We lack both ability and spirit for the highest service before we have received of the Spirit of God and yielded ourselves to do his will. Whom he calls, them he furnishes. Whom he employs, them he rewards. Piety means love, life, usefulness. God's child is a partaker of the divine nature: and that nature is life and grace. If you desire only to save your own soul—but I will not speak thus of you. You want to do good. This is the place where that good is wanted. So far as God and your neighbor are concerned, it is of more importance that you be a Christian here than in heaven: that you serve here than that you sing there. There will be no lack of celestial ministries wherever you may spend your eternity. But there is a lack of Christian men and Christian women in this world, and to-day. If you must divide your time, live for God, be a Christian here, and reserve selfishness and irreligion for the other country. Think how much piety, prolonged through many years, has had to do with the lives we venerate. Take their devotion to Christ from Matthew, and John, and Paul: and you have a tax-gatherer, a fisherman, a tent-maker. What is left which you admire when the piety of Augustine, Doddridge, Payson is removed? How the life loses its lustre and power when you take away religion from the best men you know. Let it be that they turned to God on their dying bed, and are in heaven now. How could we bless their memory but for their long years of Christian usefulness, when they showed themselves

"So anxious not to go to heaven alone!"

Oh! the world is needy, needy. It suffers for good men. It mourns for want of piety. The field is broad and white where only Christians will bear the sickle and garner the grain. If you mean to be saved, be saved to-day, that you may save others. Make your hope generous by making it alive, instant, useful. So shall it be a joy to live, and Heaven shall hail your coming, " Well done, good and faithful servant."

"Jesus of Nazareth passeth by"—not yesterday, not to-morrow—NOW. Why is he here, with bleeding hands and feet, with breaking heart? Speak to him, or ever he be gone! Say, "Lord, have mercy!" In your blindness cry, and see. In your hardness cry, and feel. In your utter need beseech the compassion which draws near to you, and know how God can bless.

# NOTHING TO DO WITH CHRIST.

### BY REV. WILLIAM WILBERFORCE NEWTON.

---

When he was set down on the judgment seat, his wife sent unto him, saying: Have thou nothing to do with that just man; for I have suffered many things this day in a dream because of him. — *Matt.* xxvii. 19.

I CALL your attention, my brethren, to the subject of this message to the Roman governor, as he sat in judgment upon it. Think for a moment of the scene! Pilate was in a sad dilemma, and did not know what he was to do with Jesus. He had given up principle and had come down to policy, and was in the midst of a miserable compromise about Barabbas, knowing that the Saviour was delivered only because of envy, when a hurried messenger, eager and impatient, came from his wife, telling him not to act at all, but only to be very skillful, and avoid doing anything. Do not let him go: that would offend the Jews. Do not pass sentence upon him, the suffering of the conscience would not hear to this. Simply let him alone, and shift all responsibility at once, by having nothing whatever to do with him. "Masterly inaction." This was the motto sent by Pilate's wife to Pilate.

Now, there is a time in every man's history when Jesus Christ stands before the judgment seat of each one of us. Christ, standing before Pilate, waiting for his decision, waiting to find out what is to be done with him,— this is only the picture of Jesus as he stands before the judgment seat of each one of us. And what is the message of the hour? What is the advice which is given to us from the spirit of this curious age? The spirit of the world sends to each one of us, in the critical epoch of each man's inner history, this same politic message: "Have thou nothing to do with that just man." The reason, too, is just the same, for the world's conscience has suffered many things, in vague, uneasy dreams, because of him. This, then, is the attitude of the thinking, bustling, unchristian world, to Christ this day. The world does not disbelieve in Christ; it dare not do this. It freely admits his claims, the fact of his existence, and the further fact of his righteous character as a just man; but then it wants to pass him entirely by, and have no relationship with him; it wants to have nothing to do with him; it wants to live in its own sphere, and act just as if there had never been any Christ, for the world has restless and uneasy dreams of Jesus, and it wants to avoid him altogether. Nothing to do with Christ! This is the motto of the world to-day. Let us look then at three phases of the world's antagonism, and at the dreams which cause this antagonism. And these three phases of the world's hostility to Christ are—the world of pleasure, and the dream of duty; the world of study, and the dream of action; and the world of man's business, and the dream of the Father's business. Each of these dreams causes suffering to the conscience. Let us look at them.

I. The world of pleasure says to the votary of pleasure, " Have thou nothing to do with that just man," for duty to Christ will not let you serve the world. So it is here the dream of duty which causes the suffering. This world of pleasure and of fashion, how very strong it is; how it gathers all its forces in battle array against the spirit of the true Christian, and exclaims, " What is the chief end of man but happiness? Let us eat and drink, for to-morrow we die." And thus it cuts with a *broad swath* upon the fresh fields of youth. Are there not times when even Nature, with her fair face, seems to woo us out of the plain path of duty? when we feel as if we could do our work if the day was disagreeable and stormy; but with such a fascinating sky, and such pure, delicious air, it seems hard and cruel to be compelled to mount an office stool, or stand at a desk, or sit through the long-drawn hours of the day, in some dull and dusty room, while all God's other creatures, in the lower range of animal life, enjoy the open day, and accomplish the purposes for which they were made in the free, untrammeled sunshine! And then, from the haggard woman in her attic, singing "Stitch, stitch, stitch" over her allotted task, to the drone, dying in the unsatisfactoriness of his satiety, we say, "Why is all this? Wherefore this perpetual antagonism? What is duty? Why can I not do as I please?" And if God's world even seems to lead us sometimes into temptation, is it surprising, with hearts bent on pleasure within us, and the world's capabilities of pleasure tempting us without, that the many in the world seek after pleasure, and the few hold on to duty? I think not, my brethren. The world is lovely, and fascinating, and bewitching, to those who have great capacities for joy, and touch the polygon of life at many points. The temptations of Satan and of sin come to us in most powerful combinations. By every avenue of the senses, by sight and sound and scent, by influence, and by example, they appeal to the sensuous nature in man, and, pushing up their appeals to the very hilt, become at last our familiar companions, and abide with us. And thus the cry goes up from the votary of pleasure in the dizzy ball-room, where everything exalts the senses, What is the use of living otherwise? What does it all amount to? Let me have nothing to do with Christ and his strict claims upon me! "What have I to do with thee, Jesus, thou Son of David? Art thou come to torment me before my time?"

My brethren, if we could rest here, if we could ask

these questions and be satisfied to go without an answer, then the Saviour might leave us to ourselves; but side by side with every wish for a life of careless pleasure there is the germ of a dream of duty. Right by the side of every strong *I will*, there is the confronting strong *I ought*. Right by the side of that which is willful and emotional, leading to carelessness and sin, there is that which is moral and conscience-stricken, trying to lead us back to God. Just when we feel most disposed to say, "I will have nothing to do with it because I want to rush into the world of pleasure," then it is that we suffer many things because of him, in the uneasy dreams of duty which will not let us slumber so; dreams which tell us of a necessity there is in the conscience and in the moral world, as well as of the freedom there is in the purely voluntary acts of the human will. It may be a nightmare dream of duty which frightens some men at last into Christianity; and yet there never was a soul that came unwillingly to Jesus; there was perfect conscious freedom about it. There is never any somnambulism about conversion, any unconscious walking in your sleep to Christ and to heaven. A dream may start men to him, but there must be a waking-time after the dream, if they are to act at all and do anything.

And so I say there are dreams of duty which at last will awaken the sleeping souls of men, and will make them realize that there is a world of eternal reality hidden beneath the encrusting world of evanescent show: that there can be a life of whole-souled Christian earnestness in that unaroused nature which is now covered by the gay drapery of the life of the thoughtless worldling; and that there is a happiness in the simple life of sincere and dutiful obedience which is better and more satisfactory as years press thick upon us, and as we grow nearer that world which cometh after this, than the conventional unnaturalisms of that life of pleasure, which with its lust of the eyes, and its lust of the flesh, and its pride of life, is not of the Father but is of that world which with all its satellites is one day to pass away forever.

There are two great wills in the world: the will of God and the will of self. The one means submission here and happiness hereafter; and the other means, from first to last, pure and unmixed selfishness. All sins can be traced to selfishness as the root and fountain head of all wrong-doing. So then the philosophy of this discrepancy between what we wish and what we ought to wish is just this: We want in this world above everything else to have our own wills; this will lead us into thorough selfishness, the constant pleasing of self, hence absolute pleasure. If, however, we sincerely want to do God's will, this will lead us into absolute submission, or Christliness, hence duty.

In the future, when sin is done away, there will be only one will again, as there was in God's sight in heaven before man was upon earth. There can never then be any antagonism between the creature and the Creator again. The two wills will run in harmony; the cry of the redeemed nature will forever be, "Have thou nothing to do with self-will; you have suffered too much in your past history upon earth because of that." Duty itself will then be pleasure; there will never be any balancing between what we wish and what we ought to wish, and so the hostility which comes from the antagonism of the world of pleasure will be finally removed, and will fade utterly away, because there will not be any world of pleasure which is not at the same time a world of duty. Then we shall indeed be changed, for then every action will be found to have something to do with Christ, for his will, which will then be ours, will cleanse and hallow everything we do.

II. And then comes the second phase of the world's antagonism to Christ, its desire to have nothing to do with him. And this is when the world of thought and mental exercise is so thoroughly satisfied with itself, that it will not listen to the dream of Christian action. Let me explain this: The world of mental temptation lies on a higher plane than the world of mere sensuous temptation. The man who does not care a straw for the pleasures of the ball-room or the stage, or the dissipations of club life, may yet hear the intellectual world he lives in whispering to him, "Have thou nothing to do with that Just Man," and he may as thoroughly obey its commands as the weaker worldling! We too often forget the sin and the temptation in certain courses of action, in the intellectual glory, which, like a halo round the moon, makes more of a show, perhaps, than the simple moon itself, but nevertheless shows it to be in an abnormal state. The halo which hangs around a temptation can never destroy the character of that temptation; the glory which lightens up a sin because it is a great man's sin can never wipe out the essentially evil character of that man's action. The spendthrift's taste leads him to the low level of the spendthrift's sin. The votary of fashion's taste leads him to a higher level, but still a level of mere indifferentism to Christianity! And the unbelieving student of art, or literature, or science, who detaches the world of thought he lives in from Christianity, and unships the compass of his life and wishes from the life and wishes of Jesus Christ,— the divine pilot of our shipwrecked human nature,— is as great a sinner in God's sight, as any one else who acts more openly by the same rule and has nothing to do with Christ. So do not point to the intellectual glory of the great man and say, "Never mind about his actions; see, what glorious thoughts!" Thought-power alone never accomplished anything in the world's history. Christ's mercy, though it existed from the beginning as a great fountain-head of ideal love and power, never would have reached us, had it not flowed out through the runnel-pipes of action. All that Jesus could have taught us would not have availed us anything if he had not done something for us, as well as taught us the truth. So when the art-student says, "I want to think and live in an ideal world, and Christianity says I must live and work in an actual world, therefore I must part from Christianity," he sins against his God; for it is the dream of action that makes him say, "I will have nothing to do with it."

So with the man of science and the man of literature, with the poet and the painter and the musician. The fine arts have ever striven to be free, and to live in a world of their own. They have always kicked against the prickings of conscience, and it is only here and there in the world's history that a sanctified genius has arisen, to show that the world of art and beauty can safely swing upon the hinges of Christianity. It is so fascinating to light the fire on your hearth, and draw the curtains, and shut out the world, and the storms and wet weather of the world, and live for thought and study alone. It is so much easier to *think* beautiful thoughts than to *do* them; to read and admire the actions of others rather than to go out in the cold and snow and accomplish the same things ourselves! It is so easy a thing to love to read the lives of the saints, and so very hard to be faithful in looking after the poor at our very door without soon tiring of it; it is so easy to talk about the Christian life, and so very difficult to practice it week after week, and year after year, without faltering in our path and growing weary in our work, or doing or saying hosts of things of which we are heartily ashamed. Think of the ideal poet, Shelley; and the wretched, unhappy man, Shelley. Think of the wonderful dreams of the poet, Goethe. Think of the passion and the heroism and the sentiment in the rich veins of his writings, and then think of him disappearing to the shady retirement of his sequestered cottage, when his country was invaded, and helpless widows and orphans sued for their fellow-countryman's loving care.

Brethren, we are not merely that which we think, else there would be two races upon the earth; a race of men and a race of angels. We are before God only what we act. We are not what we talk in society; we are what we talk in the plain every-day matters of our life at home. Christianity, then, means action; and those who want only to think, and not to act, crawl out of the Christian life of action into the selfish life of thinking. And thus it is the dream of action which causes many men in the world to have nothing to do with Christ.

III. And then comes the third and last phase of the world's antagonism to Christ; and this is the world of man's business, monopolizing all his time and attention, because it wants him to forget the dream that there is a Father or a Father's business. This is pre-eminently a utilitarian age. A few years ago we thought we had passed entirely out of the epochs of heroism and the glory which comes from romance and heroic acts, but the strong uprising of a great people to support the government has taught us that there is yet left in our Anglo-American veins the true chivalry of knighthood's days, such as ruled in the times of baronial feudal-power, and inspired men like Sir Philip Sydney to the high emprise of noble deeds. Only, men who used to tilt a lance upon a prancing charger for some specially romantic cause, now give up the heraldry of the tournament, for the citizen's dress, and the committee room.

Prince Arthur and his Round-Table knights, if they lived in these days, would form themselves into a league for the support of the administration. It is the atmosphere of the age to reduce everything to the low level of the utilitarian. And thus it is that men come into manhood from boyhood, and, forgetting their early dreams of youth, sink pleasure and study and every other thing, in the all engrossing prospect of financial success, and say of everything but money, What is the use, what does it profit? And so they run after dollars and cents as the incarnation of all power, for quoth they, "What will not money do; and if I only can have money shall I not, with it, also possess all things?" It does seem certainly a great result in life to amass a fortune and be a merchant prince among the merchants. It must be fascinating beyond measure to be able to sign one's name to a blank check and have the money ready at one's hand. Such an one is thoroughly in sympathy with the age we live in, who is able to do this. The world seems wondrously real and abiding to him. He has no difficulty about any want of faith in himself or in the men around him. Christ need never say to any of the worshipers in the temple of Mammon, "How is it that ye are so fearful, oh, ye of little faith?" It is all real and plain and useful there. Money means power; it is the secret spring of strength; but its whole range is bounded by the circumference of utility. And when a man is fairly out in business life, and sees before him a future full of promise, and is not very far off from that haven of a successful retirement where he fain would be, then comes the thought of death as a damper upon his glowing enthusiasm. Then comes the dream of another life, and an unknown future; the unwelcome dream of a Heavenly Father and a Heavenly Father's business.

It is the thought of action and earnest engrossing occupation which causes this. What is coming in the future? Is there a real life there; if so, how am I acting? How does my life here fit me for my work there? And thus when a man insists upon banishing the thoughts of a future: when he will sink the life to come in the life which now is, he lives and moves in the world, having nothing to do with Christ; it is the thought of a hereafter which drowns him in the business of the present; it is the world's success which sends like Pilate's wife this message to him: "Because of the two, hold to the one and despise the other; cling to the world of present reality and have nothing to do with Christ."

Thus, we have surveyed the three great temptations which the world of pleasure and of study and of business offer to all those who are active and enthusiastic and ambitious. The world says to each one of us, "Have thou nothing to do with Christ," for you will suffer many things in dreams because of him, if you try to serve two masters. The world of pleasure will trouble you with its dream of duty; the world of pure thought will trouble you with its dream of action; and the world of man's business will weary you with its dream of the Father's business. There is a worm at the gourd in each of them; a flaw of dissatisfaction and unrest in every mixed action, which, like the feet of Nebuchadnezzar's image, is partly iron and partly clay; partly Christian, partly not. And thus it is that the principle of the world's message is precisely the principle of our Saviour's command, "Hold to the one and forsake the other." Jesus Christ says, "Love not the world." The world says, "Have nothing to do with Christ."

My Christian brethren, one word to you. We are continually meeting men around us, and often have intimate dealings with them, who are not Christians. You meet them in society; you meet them in the community life of the university, and the exchange, and in the bustling corners of business, where men meet in common on the broad basis of their accepted merits, and where allowances for individual peculiarities are never made, and are elements utterly unknown.

How are we to treat them? What is our Christian profession for? Is it in fencing us in from the world, at the same time to fence out the world from us? Are we to clothe ourselves in the outer coverings of religion, and talk at our brethren from the stock of goodly words in our experience, as David chose the pebbles from his shepherd's bag, and hurled them at Goliath? No, my brethren! Not so. We must be true and manly Christian men. We must take men as we find them in the world. We must not sink our manhood in what we may be disposed to think are the requirements of a Christian profession, or else we cannot obey the apostle's injunction, and quit us like men. We must throw away all cant, not the foundation basis,—

the root of the matter, of which this is only the superficial covering,—for somehow it is hard for a true and honest man to respect a whining fellow-man, no matter how near canonization he may be in the church's calendar of sainthood.

The first step, then, is a thorough respect for one's character as a true Christian in God's sight, not in man's. The second step is to abandon those merely technical terms which we never use about the real things of every-day life. Why can you not talk to your neighbor about being a Christian in an open, manly way, and not feel yourself compelled to sidle up to the subject by degrees, and with the help of obsolete and long-buried expressions. They were meant, no doubt, to cover the needs of the soul, whereas, in reality, they too often only bind. They were invented to help forward the awakened soul, whereas they deceive men with mere talk about the externalism of the church, as an institution, and disgust men with spiritual things. Never let us be ashamed of Jesus, and his Cross, and his atoning work; we glory in all these! Only, if the Gospel needs translating and explaining, let us translate it into the honest language of to-day. Do not wrap it up and dwarf it in the phraseology of the past. Let us tell the old, old story of the Cross, as Jesus would tell it, if he were here on earth in this nineteenth century, to-day; just as he told it to suit the common wants of a sin-stricken world, when he was here eighteen hundred years ago.

And now does any one say, "Well, what after all is the Gospel? What shall a man do to be saved? Is there anything different; anything new-fashioned about it, in these days?" Listen, and I will tell you:

> "I say to thee, do thou repeat
> To the first man thou mayest meet
> In lane, highway, or open street—
>
> "That he, and we, and all men move
> Under a canopy of love—
> As broad as the blue sky above.
>
> "That doubt and trouble, fear and pain
> And anguish,—all are shadows vain,
> That death itself, shall not remain!
>
> "That weary deserts we may tread,
> A dreary labyrinth may thread,
> Through dark ways, underground, be led;
>
> "Yet, if we will one Guide obey,
> The dreariest path, the darkest way,
> Shall issue out in heavenly day;
>
> "And we, on divers shores now cast,
> Shall meet, our perilous voyage past,
> All in our Father's house at last!
>
> "And ere thou leave him, say thou this
> Yet one word more: they only miss
> The winning of that filial bliss
>
> "Who will not count it true that love,
> Blessing, not cursing, rules above;
> And that in it we live and move.

" And, one thing further, make him know
That to believe these things are so,
This firm faith never to forego,

" Despite of all which seems at strife
With blessing; all with curses rife,—
That this is blessing: this is life."

Let me tell you one text which has the whole Gospel in it, after all, even though we may not believe all the inferences certain theologians have drawn from it. It is this: "No man can come unto me unless the Father which hath sent me draw him." You must pray for that drawing power to lighten upon your soul. God, the Spirit's power, must take hold upon you, and grapple with your sins and with your old nature, before you can truly come to Christ with any motive that is worth anything in the way of successful Christian results. I cannot tell you how this revelation is to come to you. It may flash upon you suddenly, as the lightning does, or it may dawn upon you slowly, as the morning dawns. But it will surely come if you seek it, and pray for it. Just as the heavy water-spout breaks, in drenching columns, when a gun is fired at sea ; just as the Alpine avalanche slides its snow-fields into the yawning glaciers, when the mountain cannon breaks the stillness of the atmosphere with its reverberating echo, so your deadness must be broken ; something must start you, something must give way, if you are not to sleep on, untouched in your sins, forever! Arise, and call upon Jesus Christ, and there will then at least be a beginning. But if you keep Christ at the judgment seat of your own mind, waiting for your final decision; if you tarry for the world to send you its message, and if that message to you is that which Pilate's wife sent to Pilate,—"Avoid action altogether," "Have thou nothing to do with that just man,"—then you must share the fate of Pilate, since you make his choice. Oh! choose now, between the friendship of the world and the deep heart-love, the infinite compassion of Jesus, your Saviour, and have courage, like a man, to say "No" to the temptations of the world, when it urges you to avoid action altogether, and sends to your yielding, hesitating soul the anxious message of the Roman Governor's wife, "Have thou nothing to do with that just man, for I have suffered many things this day in a dream because of him."

# THE DOOR OPENED AND CHRIST WITHIN.

**BY REV. HENRY M. GROUT.**

---

Behold, I stand at the door and knock; if any man hear my voice and open the door, I will come in to him and will sup with him, and he with me. — *Rev.* iii. 20.

THE person from whose lips these words proceed is the Lord Jesus.

Turning to "see the voice that spake," the seer beheld one like unto the son of man, wonderful in appearance, and pre-eminent in dignity, authority, power and grace. Not only is he the faithful witness, the first-begotten of the dead, the prince of the kings of the earth, but the Son of God, the Lord, the Almighty. Having loved us and washed us from our sins, and made us kings and priests unto God, he pledges to him that overcometh, not only a crown of life, but "to sit with him in his throne."

From such lips, language like that of the text is very wonderful. The door referred to must be that of individual hearts.

I. There are hearts, then, into which Christ has as yet found no entrance. He is near, is at the very door, has made his nearness felt, and yet he is still without.

Now, this is far from true of those only whose fortune it has been to be born in a heathen land. Doubtless among such there may be those who, of dimmer light, have made more faithful use. When they come from the east and the west and the north and the south and sit down in the kingdom of God, who knows how many such will put the unbelief of more favored ones to shame? It is recorded that Christ came unto his own, and his own received him not. So it is now. In the most Christian communities, not a few live regardless of his claims and benefits. Not a few think of him as an austere man, a hard master, an uncomely root out of dry ground.

But just what is it to have Christ within? It is not merely to be familiar with the story of his life, nor to be interested in speculations concerning his nature, nor to make account of his moral precepts, nor yet to bear, and glory in, his name. In his visit to our earth he was moved by one desire which rose superior to every other. He took our nature, lived and taught, suffered and died, rose again and reascended where he was before, all for a special purpose. And he has himself declared what that was. "For the Son of man is come to seek and to save that which was lost."

Hence the names he bore. He was Immanuel, *God with us;* Jesus, *Saviour;* Christ, *the Lord.* To have received him is affectionately to have received him as divine Saviour and Lord: and to be living in the experience of those benefits he came to procure and impart. It is to have received forgiveness for past sins, and begun that new life, strength for which is from him alone.

Do you often think what it is not to have Christ within? "To as many as received him gave he power to become the sons of God." Not to have received him, then, is not to be of God's spiritual family. He is "in the believer the hope of glory." Not in you, then, you must be destitute of such a hope. To be without Christ is to be a stranger to the covenants of promise, having no hope and without God in the world. Is it not well to ponder these things? Is it not well to consider whether, for the sake of peace and safety, of present well-being and future good, one should not desire, above all else, to have Christ within?

II. But it can never be said that he is without of his own choice. The representation of Scripture, of his own lips indeed, is that he desires that it should be otherwise. "Behold," he says, "I stand at the door and knock." That is, he uses means to arrest attention, and to move men to bid him welcome.

There is a feeling, on the part of some, that though

Christ is the sinner's hope, and was willing, as the captain of our salvation, to be made perfect through suffering, nevertheless he now stands afar off, and half indifferently waits for us to take the first steps. Do you need to be reminded that that is not the gospel representation? The teaching of that is, that the indifference and unwillingness are on our part; that, as he once came a great way that he might get down to our low estate and bear our sins, so now he continues to come, and that often, and lingers, nay, tarries long, that, having gained an entrance, he may complete in us the work of salvation.

Note the great variety, as well as the fitness, of the means he is seen to employ to arrest attention; the multiplied ways in which he may be said to knock at the door of human hearts. To awaken the multitude on the day of Pentecost, he filled the Apostles with the Holy Ghost, and made them speak with other tongues. To arouse the jailer at Philippi he sent an earthquake. Saul of Tarsus was smitten down by a blinding light from heaven. But quite as often, oftener we believe, the means employed were of a less marvelous and startling nature. To the many, he came by the simple rehearsal of the story of who Jesus was, and what he had suffered and done. It was Jesus, knocking, which made Felix tremble when Paul reasoned of righteousness, temperance, and a judgment to come; which the Ethiopian heard in

Philip's question: "Understandest thou what thou readest?" and which arrested Lydia's heart as she attended unto the things that were spoken of Paul.

Nor is there less diversity in the way by which he now makes his nearness felt. Thomas Chalmers was first thoroughly aroused by the death of a friend, and an illness which well-nigh carried himself to the grave. Luther was awakened by a providence similar to the first, and a thunderbolt which fell at his feet. John Angell James, when a youth, was effectually moved by the sight of a fellow-apprentice, daring in the presence of other lodgers in the same room, to kneel at his bedside for silent prayer. A child's question, "Why do not you love Jesus?" and that of an ignorant laborer, "Sir, cannot you, too, say a word for Christ?" the one addressed to an open infidel and the other to a skeptical lawyer, afterwards a widely-honored minister, proved in each case to be the voice of the Heavenly Seeker. It is told of a worldly and careless woman, troubled about many things, but neglectful of the one thing needful, that, being alone in her room one night, the going out of the lamp which lighted it left her in darkness. Involuntarily and half aloud she said, "There is no oil in the lamp." The echo of her own words startled her. "Yes!" she added, after a moment's pause, "in the lamp of my heart there is no oil: what shall I do when the Master comes and others go in to the upper feast?"

So, whatever awakens sober thought of the uncertainty of life, and the nearness of God, of the value of the soul and the need of preparation for the life to come, may be regarded as of the nature of that knocking of which Christ speaks. Loud and alarming, or gentle and persuasive, all serve the same gracious purpose. Those chidings of conscience you may so often have wished would be silent; that death of a friend which brought the possibility of your own so vividly before you; the invitations and reminders of those whose solicitude has sometimes half provoked your impatience; the sermons and prayers and hymns you hear in the house of God; thoughts of sin and need, of duty and responsibility, of death and what is beyond, which come you know not whence nor how, are not of chance. Each and all, they tell you that Christ is at the door, and eager to come in.

III. Observe, now, the purpose of the Saviour in seeking entrance to the heart; what comes of giving him a welcome. "I will come in to him, and sup with him, and he with me."

First of all, this coming in of Christ, to sup with us and we with him, signifies peace. It has been said that to eat of another's salt, or bread, is to be safe with him, and bound to do him no hurt; that it was for this reason that David counted it so bitter and wicked a thing when Ahithophel, "*He that ate of my bread*," went over to Absalom; that, when the Jews, having offered a sacrifice, feasted on the remaining flesh, it was to show that, expiation having now been made, God and the worshiper were at peace. To give and receive hospitality has ever been looked upon as an expression of mutual regard. To sup together is to be in relations of friendship and favor.

And nothing is plainer than that this experience of conscious love to God and of being loved by him, is peculiar to those who have opened to him the door of the heart. It is quite true that he regards the most indifferent, nay, hardened and obstinate, with great compassion. God so loved the *world* that he gave his only-begotten son. Christ so loved the *world* that he humbled himself and became obedient unto death. But this is the love of pity. It is compassion yearning to do us good, not willing that any should perish: quite a different thing, as you perceive, from the love of approbation, or the look of complacency and favor. Viewed as capable of enjoyment and misery, Christ looks upon all with unspeakable tenderness. Viewed as cherishing sin, refusing to part with it, he cannot but regard such as reject his offered grace and help, with frowns of displeasure. But no sooner does the sinner break with sin and open the door to him who came to save from its curse and power, than this frown is changed to an approving smile. Doubtless the form of the Saviour's words, "Sup with him and he with me," is intended to indicate this mutual reconciliation and regard. The Saviour is glad to come in. The relenting heart is glad of his incoming.

Nor is this mutual gladness short-lived. When certain came to Jesus asking, "Lord, how is it that thou wilt manifest thyself unto us and not unto the world?" he made answer, "If any man love me he will keep my words, and I and my Father will love him, and we will come unto him and make our abode with him." That is, he comes to abide. Let me beg those, who may trust that they are entering upon a new life, not to forget that converse with Christ, much speaking with him, the frequent outgoings of thought and heart to him as one who is near and trusted and desired, all that we mean by fellowship with him, and by union as of the branch to the vine, are included in the experiences of those who have truly thus begun to live. Henceforth yours is to be a life hid with Christ in God. In that heart of yours, once filled with earth and self and sin, you have made room for him. He is now there. And it is because he is there, not because you are yourself so resolute and strong, that you are something other than what you were. Take care, therefore, to renew each day those expressions of welcome which you uttered when he was first received. Take care to ask of him the daily supplies needed to make you steadfast and strong, as well as peaceful and glad. Chalmers tells us that, before conversion, he felt himself in bondage, but afterwards his soul was unfettered as a soaring bird. Others have made use of the same figure, testifying that, having opened the whole being to Christ, the now free, strong and joyous spirit has felt itself not unlike the bird that has escaped the net, and springs exultant on the wing.

A remarkable story is told by the late Dr. Bushnell of an underwitted person, generally taken for an idiot, who, in addition to his natural disadvantages, was deep in the vices of profanity and drunkenness. In a time of religious awakening, this forlorn being came to inquire the way of salvation. Straightway he became a subject of mirth among the light-minded; while Christian people looked upon him with more of pity than hope. And yet, from that hour, on through succeeding years, he was manifestly a new creature. To his old vicious habits he never yielded an inch. He was an example of constancy and consistency to many. He wore out more than one Bible by faithful use. He saved of his earnings, for objects of Christian benevolence. When asked by his friends to explain what was, to all, so great a wonder, how it was that profanity and drunkenness never once got an advantage of him, his uniform reply was: "Why, I have seen Jesus." The incoming of Christ means power as well as peace. It means power so to live and walk, and so at last to die, as not to fail of a sight of him in his glory, and of a place at his right hand.

IV. It remains to note the condition of all this true good. That Christ may come in, what is there for us, on our part, to do? Some of you may be deeply interested in this inquiry. I would that this were the case with many, for the answer is neither difficult, nor afar off. It is right before us, and very simple: "If any man open the door!"

Seemingly, the language employed in the Scriptures to show how a sinner lost becomes a sinner saved, is extremely varied. It is, "Repent and be converted, that your sins may be blotted out;" "Ye shall seek me, and find me, when ye shall search for me with all the heart;" "Believe in the Lord Jesus Christ, and thou shalt be saved;" "Ask, and ye shall receive;" "Sell that thou hast, and give;" "Take my yoke upon you;" "Whosoever of you forsaketh not all that he hath, cannot be my disciple." One's first thought is likely to be that here is not only great variety, but confusion, nay, contradiction. Very far from this, however, is the truth. Addressed to minds in different states, they are but different ways of saying one and the same thing. To a thirsty child, standing by a fountain, cup in hand, it would be enough to say, "Dip and drink." But, if the cup were already filled with something worthless, but greatly prized, the address would take some other form: "Deny yourself; be earnest; that imagined treasure must be cast away." When it is said, "If any man hear my voice, and open the door," all that may be implied, which was expressed in the varied language just quoted. You repent that Christ has so long been kept without; for his sake are ready for any self-denial to which he may call you; believe that he is near, and all that he claims to be; and are willing that he should rule in your heart and life, as well as enrich you with treasure and gracious power. And it is because of this, that you are now, at length, ready to say,

> "Come in, come in, thou blessed one,
> Who can resist such grace!"

That is, in thought and heart, you do precisely what you would, in outward act, were some friend you had wronged and resisted, now at the door of your dwelling.

"Oh!" you say, "but this is too simple." No, it is not too simple. And it is to be feared that it is neither the simplicity nor the difficulty of the way that keeps the many from it. "But," you reply, "I have often said, Come in! I am saying it now; I wish him to enter and take possession." Do you mean all this? Are you dealing honestly with yourself? Consider a moment. Is it not possible that, so far from having made room and swung wide the door, your heart is so crowded with things you are not willing to have cast out, that for such a visitor there is no place? More than this; heaps of rubbish may crowd against the door so that love, even so powerful as his, cannot force an entrance. There, for instance is your pride, an unwillingness to go out and have it known that henceforth you belong to him; your self-righteousness, a persuasion you cannot surrender that your moral virtues and many upright and noble qualities deserve divine reward; your ambition and love of earthly pleasure, eagerness for power or place or gratification of sense, which you are not quite ready to exchange even for all the riches of Christ. So far from having opened the door, these may be piled against it. The sinner, praying for the grace of salvation, is very often like the man who, while saying to a friend, "Come in!" should, with his whole strength, be holding the door lest his invitation be accepted; the louder he calls, the more firmly he braces. In some sense, such an one does want the Saviour. But, in no sense does he want him just yet. At best, the meaning of all his prayer is, as Augustine so long cried: "Lord, cleanse me, but not now!"

In closing, let me remind you, then, that Christ does not force himself upon any heart. You must cease resistance, cast out the rubbish, and open the door. He comes very near. He waits patiently and long. He knocks often, sometimes very hard. He takes many ways to remind you of his nearness and love. But you must yourself consent to receive him. Preferring him to your sins, to your best treasure, to your standing in society, to your chief delights and highest ambitions, to your dearest friend, you must cordially and honestly bid him enter and take possession. Can you not do this? Can you not do it to-day; this hour; this moment?

There is one phrase here which we have not yet emphasized: "If *any* man hear my voice." You may think yourself too old, too young, too wise, too ignorant, too sinful, or too good. Christ says, "If *any* man!" He means *you*.

# FAITH THE SOURCE OF FAITHFULNESS.

**BY REV. JOSEPH COOK.**

---

Sanctified by Faith. — *Acts* xxvi. 18.

Who are faithful? Those who have faith. What is faith? That which makes a man faithful.

When faith is discussed we ought to listen first, midst, and last, to the intonations which came to Paul out of a light bright above the brightness of the noon; for in all the Scriptures there is no proclamation as to the nature and the necessity of faith more mysteriously majestic and hallowed than the meridian words, our Lord's own, constituting Paul a teacher of the globe in religion. After receiving a fathomless message from the Unseen Holy, Paul "was not disobedient to the heavenly vision," but taught first at Jerusalem and then at Athens, Corinth, and Rome, repentance, faith, and the sanctification which is the result of both. We must never forget that our Lord had many things to say to his disciples after he left the world; and that this supreme proclamation of the necessity of faith made to Paul when his apostleship began, is a proclamation equally for you and me here in Boston to-night. Many of us have a kind of faith that does not sanctify us. In exhibiting faith as the source of faithfulness, I wish to be very elementary; and therefore I must speak from human example, in order that, drawing nigh in the light of dawn, we may not at first sight be dazzled by the glory of the Atonement until we are bewildered, as many a philosopher has been in Boston and elsewhere.

On the slope of Beacon Hill, a New England author, who ought always to be named side by side with Pestalozzi, once made it a rule, in a school full of subtle thought, that if a pupil violated its regulations the master should substitute his own voluntary sacrificial chastisement for that pupil's punishment. Bronson Alcott, were he here, would allow me to say, as I have said publicly in his presence elsewhere, that he has told me that that one regulation almost Christianized his school. The pupils were quite young, and for that reason the measure was effective among them. He was no dreamer. He would never have adopted this measure except with the sensitive. Nevertheless, the operation of these untutored, hardly unfolded, and, therefore, unstained hearts indicated what man is. "One day," says Bronson Alcott, "I called up before me a pupil of eight or ten years of age, who had violated an important regulation of the school. All the pupils were looking on, and they knew what the rule of the school was. I put the ruler into the hand of that offending pupil; I extended my hand; I told him to strike. The instant the boy saw my extended hand and heard my command to strike I saw a struggle begin in his face. A new light sprang up in his countenance. A new set of shuttles seemed to be weaving a new nature within him. I kept my hand extended, and the school was in tears. The boy struck once, and he himself burst into tears. I constantly watched his face, and he seemed to be in a bath of fire, which was giving him a new nature. He had a different mood toward the school and toward the violated law. The boy seemed transformed by the idea that I should take chastisement in place of his punishment. He went back to his seat, and ever after was one of the most docile of all the pupils in that school, although he had been at first one of the rudest." This story does not come from Greece. It is actual history in Boston. That is the way human nature is made in New England, here on Beacon Hill; and my impression is that human nature is just the same everywhere. If Bronson Alcott had done that with a Greek boy, the effect would have been the same. It would have been the same with a Brahmin boy, a Negro boy, or an Esquimaux boy.

Now, will you be so kind, my most restless and unbelieving friends, as to take a little arc of the moral law revealed to you in this example and extend it through the whole circumference of the circle? You say that law is a unit everywhere. You say that physical law is the same here and among the stars. You say that if you know what gravitation is here, you know what it is in the North Star. But, if physical law is the same thing everywhere, moral law is the same thing everywhere. If you, standing on the atom we call earth, can take a little arc of the physical law and estimate what that law is everywhere, you may take a little arc of the moral law and estimate what that is everywhere; and you are just as scientific in the last act as in the first. So our Lord assumes in his parables that the moral law is the same everywhere. Therefore it is not enough for me to say that this boy would have been affected just as he was if he had been a Greek or an Italian or an Esquimaux boy. Undoubtedly, any free being anywhere in the universe would have been affected in just that way. I cannot think that the moral law is so very different in other worlds, that I have not the right to draw an inference as to what it is there from its operation here, by extending the circumference of it from any arc I can accurately measure. Assuredly, under that discipline it was natural for the boy to be moved as he could not be in any other way. Moved to what? Moved to shame, in view of his own transgressions; moved to reverence of and love for the master; moved to loyalty to that rule which he had broken.

People say that all illustrations of the Atonement are imagination, or taken out of some doubtful corner of the newspapers; but, if you please, this occurred in Boston, among the philosophers, and to a Concord philosopher. I have tears sometimes, and sometimes groans, for that style of unrest which will not believe the deep instincts of the soul; which draws down upon itself God's supreme curse of blindness, because it refuses to follow the light it has, and which, by sinning against that light, loses half the light it possesses. I affirm that we all know that it is natural for human nature, looking on the chastisement of a ruler for the punishment of the subject, to feel two things: first, that the violation of the law is not excused, or that there is no letting down of the dignity of the law at all; and secondly, that there could not be brought to bear upon the rebellious subject any motive so likely to win him to loyalty as that substitution of the ruler's chastisement for the punishment of the subject. There is surely nothing known to philosophy, or imagination, or to human experience, that takes hold of the soul like that. This is a fact. It is just as much a fact as anything about geological strata. It is just as hard a fact, and will bear the microscope and the scalpel just as well. We are made so that such a sight takes hold of us. I am not asking now whether an Atonement has ever been made; but I do say that if one has been made on that principle, then that is what we want, for that is what will take hold of us as nothing else can. That is what is to be held up above all philosophy; that is what is to be placed over Beacon Hill and the North End. That is what is to be told over and over, in all ways, until men, gazing on that spectacle, are transformed by the gaze into loyalty—into glad allegiance to their Saviour as their King. My friends, I am not ashamed of the power of that natural law which lies behind what we call the principle of the Atonement. I am not ashamed of the Cross of Christ, for it is a part of the nature of things. It is not an insertion into the universe to correct mistakes. It is not an afterthought. Law is a unit throughout the whole extent of time and space; and if you can measure a little arc of the moral law as exhibited in this school of the Concord philosopher, you will obtain some glimpse of the principle on which the Atonement operates; for the definition of the Atonement is the substitution of the voluntary sacrificial chastisement of Christ for man's punishment.

Why do I make a distinction between chastisement and punishment? Because facts require me to do so. In this example was Bronson Alcott punished? Not at all. Was Bronson Alcott guilty? Not at all. Was the personal demerit of that pupil transferred to Bronson Alcott? Not at all. Such transference of personal demerit is an impossibility in the nature of things. Nevertheless, we have in Boston a school of theology and preaching, and a wide range of popular sentiment, which regards Christianity as teaching in the doctrine of the Atonement a self-contradiction, an absurdity — namely, the idea that personal demerit is transferred from one individual to another.

James Martineau says that the idea of a vicarious Atonement is abhorrent to him, because it includes the assertion that Christ, an innocent being, was punished. I wish to admit that orthodoxy has been careless in her phrases again and again. I do not know how many have been thrown into the lawless license of liberalism by that misconception of the Atonement which assumes that in it an innocent being was punished and personal demerit was transferred. But law is one through the universe, and I have a perfect right to stand on this example of Alcott's school. I affirm that you know perfectly well that Bronson Alcott, in the strict sense, did not suffer punishment. He was innocent. What did happen? Bronson Alcott voluntarily accepted chastisement, not punishment. What is the definition of punishment? Pain inflicted for personal blameworthiness. What is chastisement? Pain suffered for the improvement of the one who suffers it, or for the benefit of those who witness it. Does the latter imply guilt? Not at all. A mother has a vicious son, and she has done her duty by him, let us suppose. She has no remorse, for I assume she is free from all guilt for her son's bad habits; but she suffers terribly. Is that pain punishment? No; chastisement. We must make this distinction in Boston, at least, where so long the caricature has been placarded on the highest walls, asserting that in the Atonement punishment is inflicted on an innocent being and personal demerit transferred. I never was taught that Christ suffered punishment. I had to learn out of books that any one made it an objection to Christianity that an innocent being was punished. If religious science will begin the fashion, and never use a term of importance without defining it, I, for one, will try to keep step with that fashion as one of the most blessed of all modern improvements, and one I should like to force, by the contagion of general acceptance, upon all who differ from Christian views. The chastisement of our offenses was laid upon our Lord. It is nowhere presumed in the Scriptures that personal demerit can be transferred from individuality to individuality.

It is self-evident that personal ill-desert cannot be removed from person to person.

What! Sin not taken off us and put upon our Lord? Our guilt not borne by our Saviour? No; not in the sense in which you understand guilt. Blameworthiness is not transferred from us to him, and can not be. We know that our Lord had no sin, and that there can be no taking off personal ill-desert from one personality and putting it upon another. That word guilt is a fog unless you remember that behind it lie two meanings. Guilt signifies, first, personal blameworthiness; second, obligation to render satisfaction to violated law. In the former sense guilt can not be transferred from person to person. In the latter it can be. Our Lord is no murderer; no perjurer. There is no divergence of theological opinion from self-evident truth when self-evident truth declares that personal demerit is not transferable from personality to personality. Ghastliest of all misconceptions ever put before this city, or any other, is the assertion that the doctrine of the Atonement implies, first, that an innocent being is made guilty in the sense of being personally blameworthy; and secondly, that that innocent being is punished in the sense of suffering pain for personal ill desert. Both these propositions all clear thought discards, all religious science condemns. We have no doctrine of the Atonement which declares that personal demerit is laid upon our Lord, or that, in the strict sense of the word, he suffered punishment, —that is, pain inflicted for personal blameworthiness. He had no personal blameworthiness. He was an innocent being—as he always will be—and never did, can, or will suffer punishment, in the strict sense of the word.

Guilt—in the second sense, or obligation to satisfy the demands of a violated law—may be removed when the Author of the law substitutes his own voluntary sacrificial chastisement for our punishment.

When such a substitution is made, the highest possible motives to loyalty to that Ruler are brought to bear upon the rebellious subject.

If any great arrangement on this principle has been made by the Father, Redeemer, and Sanctifier of the universe, that arrangement meets with exactness the deepest wants of man. It is the highest possible dissuasive from the love of sin; and it is the only possible deliverance from the guilt of sin, in the sense not of personal blameworthiness, but of obligation to satisfy the violated law which says "I ought."

*Such a great arrangement may, therefore, with scientific exactness be known to be needed, and so needed as to be called properly the desire of all nations.*

The Atonement which reason can prove is needed, Revelation declares has been made.

It is perfectly clear, however, that more than the moral influence of the character, sufferings, and precepts of our Lord, is concerned in the Atonement. What is called the moral theory of the Atonement will not exhaust the meaning of even this human case. It is very evident that the pupil's peace before the law of the school is the result not of his own work, but of the master's work; *and not of the master's moral influence and general character merely, but of his substitution of chastisement for punishment.*

Nevertheless, the pupil must be loyal to the master; and thus, though not saved by works, cannot be saved without works.

*It is not simply the moral influence or character and general example of the master which transforms the boy into the mood of loyalty. But this substitution of voluntary sacrificial chastisement for punishment is the force which throws the shuttles that weave a new character in the soul thus delivered from punishment.* Although the record of disobedience cannot be changed, and must be remembered with regret, such memory, when loyalty is once made so perfect in love and trust as to cast out fear, will be but a spur to adoration of the condescension shown to the released soul.

What happened further in that school? Suppose that boy had been called up and punished a second time after the master had been chastised. Would that have been right? Would the school have said that was right? The master has accepted chastisement voluntarily; and now you cannot call that boy up and punish him a second time. The school would say that is wrong. It is against all human nature to do that. What has the master done? He has paid the debt of that boy to the school. But the master is not to blame? No. The master has not been punished? No. Assuredly, this case, on the human side, looks intelligible. I think I can understand that side. But do you mean to say that in the arc of that little example are involved principles that sweep the whole curve of the Atonement or show in part how God's chastisement was substituted for our punishment?

Yes, by more than a glimpse; for law is the same everywhere.

The caricature which represents the doctrine of the Atonement as demoralizing is the most miserable of all. That boy goes back to his seat at peace with the law of the school. How? By his good works? No. Without good works? No. You say it is a mystery that people teach when they say a man is not saved by good works and yet is not saved without them? That boy has violated the law; he has seen his master's chastisement substituted for his punishment, and he goes back to his seat at peace, and you cannot demand from him another payment of the debt; but would the first payment be of any value if the boy were to lose loyalty to that master? If you can suppose that the boy would disregard that supreme exhibition and fall into his old ways, do you think that he could quote the substituted chastisement as a ground of peace? It is not in natural law that he could, and it is not in Christianity that he could. It is not taught anywhere in the Bible that he could. It is taught nowhere in Scripture that men can be saved without loyalty to God as our Lord as well as our Saviour.

You say that the Bible says, "Believe on the Lord Jesus Christ and be saved." But to *believe* and *believe in* or *on* are two very different things. Many a statement of a bad man I can believe, but there is no bad man that I can *believe in*. There is a great difference between believing and believing in. I believe Congress when it makes a public statement; but I do not believe *in* all the acts of Congress—nor in all its members! I believe Benedict Arnold when he writes an autobiographical sketch; but I do not believe *in* Benedict Arnold. I believe Washington and Lincoln when they write letters, and I also believe *in* Washington and Lincoln. On the one hand we have *believing*, and on the other *believing in* or *on*, and the Greek tongue makes even a clearer distinction between the two than the English. But when the great words are cited, "Believe on the Lord Jesus Christ," how often, although this language is Biblical, does it fail to convey the meaning it always contains, of the necessity of affectionate self-commitment of the soul to God, or of rejoicing personal loyalty to him as both Saviour and Lord? Coleridge said, "I believe Plato and Socrates; I believe *in* Jesus Christ."

What is saving faith? What is the difference between belief and faith? I venture much, but I shall be corrected swiftly here if I am wrong. Saving faith, rightly defined, is—

1. A conviction of the intellect that God, or God in Christ, is, and

2. An affectionate choice of the heart that God, or God in Christ, should be both our Saviour and our Lord.

The first half of this definition is belief; the whole is faith. All of it without the last two words would be merely religiosity and not religion. There is in that definition nothing which teaches that a man is saved by opinion irrespective of character. Belief is assent, faith is consent to God as both Saviour and Lord.

On April 19, 1775, a rider on a horse flecked with blood and foam, brought to the city of Worcester the news of the battle of Lexington, in which Theodore Parker's grandfather captured the first British gun. The horse fell dead on the main street of the city; and, on another steed, the rider passed westward with his news. Some of those who heard the intelligence were loyal and some were disloyal. They all heard that there had been a victory of the American troops over the British, and they all believed the report. Now, was there any political virtue or vice in the belief by the tory in Worcester that there had been a victory over the British? Was there any political virtue or vice in the belief by the patriot yonder that there had been a victory over the enemy? Neither the one nor the other. Where, then, did the political virtue or vice come in? Why, when your tory at Worcester heard of the victory he believed the report, and was sorry, and was so sorry that he took up arms against his own people. When the patriot heard the report, he believed it, and was glad, and was so glad that he took up arms and put himself side by side with the stalwart shoulders of Parker's grandfather. In that attitude of the heart lay the political virtue or political vice. Just so in the government of the universe, we all hear that God is our Saviour and Lord, and we all believe this, and so do all the devils, and tremble. Is there any virtue or vice in that belief, taken alone? None whatever. But some of us believe this, and are sorry. We turn aside; and, although we have assent, we have no consent to God, and we take up arms against the fact that he is our Saviour and Lord. Others of us believe this, and, by divine grace, are glad; we have assent and consent both; we come into the mood of total, affectionate, irreversible self-surrender to God, not merely as a Saviour, but also as Lord. When we are in that mood of rejoicing loyalty to God, we have saving faith, and never till then. How can salvation be obtained by assent alone, that is, by opinion merely? What is salvation? It is permanent deliverance from both the love of sin and the guilt of sin. Accepting God gladly as Saviour we are delivered from the guilt of sin, and accepting him gladly as Lord we are delivered from the love of sin. Only when we accept God as both Saviour and Lord are we loyal; only when we are affectionately glad to take him as both are we or can we be at peace. When we believe the news that he is Saviour and Lord and are glad, and so glad as to face the foe, we are in safety.

In the case of that scholar in Bronson Alcott's school, guilt meant two things: first, his own personal blameworthiness; second, his obligation to do something to pay the debt owed to the school. Now, guilt in the first sense never is removed.* It is not the doctrine of the Atonement that personal demerit is taken off a man by saving faith. It was always true of that scholar that he violated the law. His personal demerit had not been transferred to Bronson Alcott at all. The record of rebellion is always behind that boy. Only his obligation to pay the debt due to the school has been removed. That latter sense of guilt is the meaning of the word when we say the Atonement removes man's guilt. *It is scientifically certain that Bronson Alcott had power to pay the debt which that boy owed, and that he paid it by substituting his own chastisement for that boy's punishment.* That is a straightforward, plain case, and you can teach any honest man to see that distinction. Hereafter, when skepticism, with its long-eared hallelujahs, comes to you and says that the Atonement is a doctrine outgrown by all clear thought, because it teaches that an innocent being was punished, and that personal demerit was transferred from one individual to another, and that, therefore, advanced thought must abandon the central idea of Christian culture as plainly barbaric, the result of some Platonic interfusion of thought in the early centuries, or some heathenish inheritance from Judaism —in short, that this scheme is self-contradictory or at

---

* Hodge's Theology. *passim.*

war with axiomatic truth, please ask that singer of empty anthems to be clear himself; to state what he would say in a human case such as I have supposed; and then whether he dare affirm, in the name of the unity of law which he proclaims as the first truth of science, that, if there has been any such Atonement made in the universe, it is not what we infinitely need.

My friends, exact and cool science knows with precision that we want just this more than unspeakably, if anything like this has been done for us. We want it, first, to pay our debt to the school of the universe, and, next, to give us immeasurable motives to loyalty. There is surely nothing that really changes the heart so quickly as a sight of this substitution of chastisement for punishment, whether it be in the human case of a school, or in the revealed case of the school of the universe. Lift this feeling of the poor boy into all the dignity it naturally assumes when you take it as a type of the moral law, a unit throughout the universe. Lift that law until the arc we can measure has become the segment of a circle large enough to reach from here to the galaxies, and then let all the constellations shine on the circle as you carry its line far past the spot over which Boötes is driving his hunting dogs in their leash of sidereal fire; carry on that arc until stars fade out, and galaxies, and all the infinities and eternities of time past and time to come are embraced within it, and then what have you? One little point of light—the whole of it is no more—to hold up before the noon of God's chastisement substituted for man's punishment.

You wish to be born anew? Look on the Cross! You wish to take God gladly as your Lord? Look on him as your Saviour. You wish to drop all the heart-burdens of slavishness and you desire to come into the obedience of delight? Look on the Cross! You want glad allegiance to God as King? Look on the Cross! There is nothing that frees us from the love of sin like looking on him who has delivered us from the guilt of it.

Speaking philosophically, addressing you in the mood of cool precision, I affirm that, if the great things man wants are riddance from the love of sin and deliverance from the guilt of it, we can obtain the first best and the latter only by looking on the Cross. Those old words have unfathomable depth; and he who is to be born anew must sit beside that pupil in Bronson Alcott's school, must imagine the benches to be the galaxies, and his human companions the angels and archangels who bow down on the golden floor, and on the shore of the sea of glass, and in presence of the Great White Throne, and cry out: "Holy, Holy, Holy Lord God Almighty, thou art worthy, for thou didst so love the world that thou gavest thine only begotten Son, that whosoever believeth on him should not perish, but have everlasting life."

On a summer evening, it has often been to me, on both sides of the Atlantic, a solemn joy to lie down alone at a grove's edge by the side of the ocean and look into the infinite azure until the stars appear. In the rustle of the grove, one may hear thus all the forests of all the zones of the thrifty, jubilant, wheeling world; the soul may touch all shores with the howling, salt, uneasy sea. As the stars come out, I love to lift above my thoughts Richter's apologue, which represents an angel as once catching a man up into the infinite of space and moving with him from galaxy to galaxy, until the human heart fainted, and called out: "End is there none of the universe of God?" and the constellations answered: "End is there none, that ever yet we heard of." Again the angel flew on with the man past immeasurable architraves and immensity after immensity, sown with rushing worlds, and the human heart fainted again and cried out: "End is there none of the universe of God?" and the angel answered: "End is there none of the universe of God: lo! also, there is no beginning." But if, while I, thus entranced, look into the sky, you bring above my gaze the page of the Gospel recording the fact of the Atonement, all other revelations of the divine glory appear in contrast but chaff and dust.

# OUR TWO HARVESTS.

### BY RUFUS ELLIS, D.D.

---

Be not deceived; God is not mocked: for whatsoever a man soweth that shall he also reap. For he that soweth to his flesh shall of the flesh reap corruption; but he that soweth to the Spirit shall of the Spirit reap life everlasting. — *Gal.* vi. 7, 8.

THE subject of my sermon is Our Two Harvests.

I. Let me say, first, that I am concerned about them because they are ours. It is true that a portion of the fruit of our life, good and bad, is not from our own sowing; but it is not true that we can ever look upon the ripening harvest of our days as one might look upon another man's husbandry, rejoicing or mourning, but with no sense of having had anything to do with it. We have had a great deal to do with it, and the more we feel our responsibility the better it will be for us.

II. And let me say again that these harvests of our life have that grave importance and kind of finality which belong to other harvests. That by which we live is at stake. There may be, there are, thank God, merciful provisions against failure, as when of old there was corn in Egypt; but a famine, whether of truth or of bread, is none the less a terrible reality, and though a starving or even a dead soul may be recovered, it is none the less a fearful thing to come into any such straits and to find ourselves, as so many do as the year of our life closes, in the midst of a bad harvest.

So much because so many say that we are what God makes us, or what our fathers make us, or what our circumstances make us, and not what we make ourselves. So much because there are so many who, believing in a good-natured God, a God who forgives, but not in a God who is just, in their uninstructed reliance upon infinite love, fail to see that the laws by which souls live and die are even more tragic in their working than what we call the laws of matter, and that God is not mocked. The Two Harvests are ours.

III. Paul gives to one of them a very evil-sounding name. He calls it a harvest of corruption, a harvest of death, and it comes, he says, from sowing to the flesh. It is what they get out of life and all they get out of it, who provide for the lower part of our nature to the neglect of the higher part. I say *to the neglect* of the higher part, because in its place the lower as well as the higher has its divine rights. And I include in the lower part of our nature the intellect and the imagination as well as the senses; I take in all that Paul means when in another place he writes of "the natural man." Very often the sowing to the flesh is a very literal sowing, and the harvest is very literally a harvest of corruption; there are those who are alive only to the senses, and their reward is a body no longer capable of enjoyment, for enjoyment long since ended in satiety and it may be agony. You see the man's wages in the dull eye, in the sodden face, in the palsied limbs. It is only the foul sepulchre of a man, however whitened and garnished; only a brute, we should say, if that were not a libel upon poor dumb creatures. Alas! upon how many human faces you see the mark of the beast, and we can only say to ourselves: How ever can this corruptible put on incorruption, and this mortal be clothed with immortality, and this death be swallowed up in victory?

But the words of the Apostle need not receive so literal an application. We may understand by corruption, characters and conditions which are without abiding worth and beauty; perishing, dissolving, vanishing, as things having no root, and yielding not the faintest suggestion of immortality or even of continuance. Paul calls this harvest corruption because it is so corruptible, because it is a fading pageant, a vain show, a dream when one awaketh. It is the outcome of life, and more and more, as time goes on, it is found to be this, not merely when a man sinks into low and debasing indulgences, but when his life centres upon himself and aims at nothing high and universal; when he keeps his eye, as the phrase is, fixed upon the main chance, and will run no risk of destroying himself by being righteous overmuch, proposing to cultivate his own intellect, to build up his own fortune, to advance his own household, nay, to save his own precious soul, come what may of other souls. How to get on in the world and get the most wages for the least work, and carry our wares to the best market, to sell when what one has to sell is the dearest, and to buy when what one has to buy is the cheapest, to say what men love to hear, to seek one's own in studies and amusements, — are aims which are compatible with the utmost delicacy and tenderness. The mind may even be great in a certain sense, and yet as low-toned and selfish as that which is sunk in coarse and gross indulgences. The only difference is that sometimes our sins go before us to judgment, and sometimes they follow after. We must not be misled by this word "corruption" into picturing only what is animal and sensual. The profligacies of the prodigal were only the accidents of the condition. It was his sin, and the cause of all other sins, that he must have his portion and do his own pleasure. With more prudence and a different temperament, and in other circumstances, he might have been reputably and not disreputably self-indulgent, as signally successful, as man too often counts success, as he was in all eyes a wretched failure. There are many whose reward for painstaking, decent, useful lives in exacting and responsible occupations includes nothing abiding, and with the advance of years, as the Bible says, "their very thoughts perish," and the world which seemed so real to them, even the only reality, begins to look unsubstantial, and into the future there is no clear outlook. Theirs was the larger share in the scramble for wealth or place; but where what we want is quality, not quantity, the smaller share would have been no more disappointing than the larger; and if it be only a feast of shells or husks, a little heap will be even less burdensome than a large one. Much laborious husbandry is rewarded with no imperishable fruit, because the sower sows only for earth and time, and poorly even so. "Verily I say unto you, they have their reward;" but is it *rewarding?* One said of certain persons who had not been successful as success is commonly understood, "They have not had a good time." Would they have had any better time if they had succeeded?

IV. But God has provided better things for us if we will have them. There is another harvest, fruit every month, from the Tree of Life, whose leaves never wither. It is theirs who sow unto the spirit, whose purpose and plan are from within and from above; who are born of the Spirit, and are alive with a diviner life; to whom God and Christ are real, and whatsoever things are pure and honorable and lovely and helpful to man are objects to be eagerly desired and laboriously sought after. This harvest of Everlasting Life includes all that man needs on earth, all that makes up success, all that distinguishes a true civilization from the miserable estate of the savage, all honorably earned wealth, culture, science, art, household refinement, all that men laboriously seek for themselves, for their children, and for their world; but these needful things are all lifted into light and made living and abiding, earthly and heavenly treasures at once; not that wealth which some coveting have strayed away from the faith and have pierced themselves through with many pangs. And in our training we ought to provide *before* all else for that which is so continually put *after* all else. It is as indispensable for a man to be twice born as to be once born; and if he cannot be twice born, he had better not be born at all; indispensable to come into the light and life of heaven, as well as into the light and life of earth. We are not men as God means us to be until we are born of the Spirit into a childhood, at least, of faith and hope and charity; not, surely, not, in Christian homes, through some spasm of amazement and terror, but as the sweet Dayspring dawns upon night and darkness, and spreads itself over an awakening world, and man goes forth to his labors and enjoyments. Our religious fathers were not one jot too earnest in their desire and purpose to waken up in the soul of youth, first of all, the everlasting life of love, that so the better nature, having obtained help from God from the start, might have some fair chance in the struggle of our life, and our whole condition be advanced and redeemed. If only we had something which might take the place, in our week-day schools, of their grand but now obsolete catechism: if only a small portion of the pains expended upon the understanding might be given to wake up and invigorate the spiritual and moral nature: if only religion could be taught like the languages and the mathematics: and whilst our children are learning so many tongues they might be guided to speak the truth in one. But only they who believe can waken and nourish belief and lift the hearts of the young into aspirations and unselfish loves and true ambition, and mostly it is done by example. We want evangelists whose chief aim it shall be so to lift young and old into the Divine Life, that they shall be ashamed and afraid to live another day, here or anywhere else, any life which is not pure and helpful and inspired, proposing generous aims, and fed by great expectations.

V. Now, to live such a life we must be alive betimes, not chiefly to the enjoyments of sense, the accumulation of riches, the achievement of earthly greatness, the success which begins and ends in time and seems to be fitly rounded by the sleep of death; we must be alive in the Bible sense, living towards all that is highest and best, alive at the very centre and core of our being with the life which is of God.

When we see a fresh and growing body, a strong and expanding mind, enterprise, energy, hope, courage in all worldly matters, and yet no signs of any moral or religious fervors, or of any desire or purpose to live above the levels of an ordinary worldliness, we can only say that the spirit is not yet born, and that in the noblest sense of the word the youth, the maiden, is not yet living. What is called the second death, the deep sleep which evil-doing pours upon the spirit, is seldom experienced by one who has ever been well alive, and most happily, for of all religious enterprises theirs is the most arduous who would call back from their graves those who have passed from spiritual life to spiritual death. It is only to repent, you say; ah! but that is just the most difficult thing in this world. "Can the Ethiopian change his skin?" It is a far easier task to second the divine pleading with the hearts of the young, to entreat them by all heavenly motives, by all high and pure examples, and chiefly by his living and dying and rising who is at once our brother and our Lord, to heed that voice which, at least as a whisper, we have all heard, and which beseeches us before all else to follow God in the way of duty and of love. Speak to that young man, to that young woman; say what is so true,—for who does not count his own life to be more a failure than a success?—that you would give all you have of fortune, or position, or name, or fame, to stand as they stand to-day in the beginning of their years at the threshold of life, with its days, few or many, all before them, and with the sense which you have now of the work which may be done, the joy which may be tasted, and the faith by which we may be fed in this time of our mortal life. Tell them of the Two Harvests, of the Harvest of Death and of the Harvest of Life; that they are the sowers and that they must be the reapers. Tell them of the God who will not be mocked, and of the God who is always faithful, and it may be the Spirit's occasion to enlarge and uplift and fill their hearts, and they shall sow unto the Spirit, and whatsoever they do shall prosper, and grace shall ripen into glory, and, being faithful unto death, they shall receive a crown of life.

# THE GOSPEL INVITATION.

### BY W. F. WARREN, D.D.

---

The Spirit and the Bride say, Come. — *Rev.* xxii. 17.

THIS little word, Come, is the keynote of the Bible, the call and catchword of all dispensations. Ever since man fell away from God, God has been calling him back. Five and twenty centuries ago it was by the lips of the venerable Isaiah. The then loud accents have grown soft and faint in the distance, but they are still distinct and musical: "Ho, every one that thirsteth, come ye, . . . come, . . . yea, come." Eighteen centuries ago, it was by the lips of his Son: "Ho, all ye that labor and are heavy-laden, come." Here in our text, the last living apostle, closing the last book of Divine Revelation, projects the same word forward into the coming ages, as the one thing never to be forgotten: "Come, and let him that heareth say, Come, and whosoever will, let him take of the water of life freely." That sweet voice of invitation is ringing on and on to-day. We all hear it. The Spirit is saying, Come. The Bride, which is the Church, is saying, Come. Every one that heareth—to purpose—becomes transformed into a new herald and cries, Come. The athirst do come, and thus this glorious Gospel of the Kingdom is getting preached in all the world for a witness to all nations.

Beloved, I stand here simply to vocalize once again this gracious call of the Spirit and Bride. Not to speculate, not to argue, not to rhapsodize,—simply to say out loud what God so often whispers in your hearts, to add the cords of a man to the drawings of the Father. I view myself simply as one more of the servants sent out by the Master of the Feast, to cry in the highways and hedges, "All things are ready. Come!"

And first of all, I fain would catch the ear of any in my audience who may be very far from the kingdom of heaven, who in heeding the call will have far to come. And who is farthest from the kingdom? Our thoughts are apt to turn to the thief, the drunkard, the harlot, to descend to those dens of crime and infamy which have been fitly termed the breathing-holes of perdition. But are these people, after all, the most hopeless subjects for God's invitation? Has not Christ rebuked such judgments in those scathing words which he addressed to the moral and highly respectable Pharisees of his time: "Behold, the publicans and harlots enter into the kingdom before you." I am inclined to think that in our land and time no class of men are farther from the kingdom than that small, intelligent, moral, and highly respected class of persons who aspire to be religious *connoisseurs*. They manifest not the least shyness in speaking of religious subjects, only this is noticeable, they are more apt to speak of religions than of religion. You, friend, yonder, are one of them. You think the religions are a most interesting study. You love to read what philologists and philanthropists have written about their origin, their laws of development, their comparative merits. You are fond of philosophizing yourself in a modest way on these lofty subjects. Christianity, you deign to say, is a very good religion, but your trouble is that it is only one of many systems, any one of which is about as good as another, and no two of which can possibly be true.

Very good. Let me ask you a question in this interesting field of research. Have you, in all your studies, ever found any other religion than the Christian which says, Come?

Allah does not say, "Come;" Allah says, rather, "Go, do this, do that, abstain from this, abstain from that." Allah is a repellant sovereign, a domineering autocrat; not a Father, bowing the heavens and beckoning his children to come to him.

Then there is Buddha. Buddha never says, "Come."

Buddha never says anything. According to his own followers he is dead; worse than that, the flame of his being has been "blown out;" Nirvana swallowed him up more than two thousand years ago. Out of that abyss of non-being no word of invitation can ever come. Even if there could, its " come " would only signify annihilation.

Here are the pantheistic religions. How is it here? Pantheism is even muter than Buddhism. Buddha did have a voice the fourscore years he lived, and did say to men, Come, but the pantheist's god never had either voice or consciousness. He is an eternal deaf-mute, hopelessly such; no deaf and dumb asylum in the world would attempt his cure. The pantheistic god is the sum total of being, and sum totals are not given to speech. When pantheism gets a god who is alive and can speak, we shall be glad to hear what he has to say; that moment, however, it will cease to be pantheism.

There was classic heathenism. Did Jupiter ever say to men, Come ? Did he ever plead with them to lay off the earthly and put on the heavenly? Did he yearn to lift them into fellowship with himself, to make them sharers of his divine nature, co-occupants of the heavenly Olympus? You know he never did. You know he never sought to draw humanity to his bosom and bless it. On the contrary, he was from the beginning the sworn foe of humanity. He was jealous of human happiness, and grudged men the simplest blessings. Take their own story of him. Our infant race was shivering in the frigid earth, perishing. Prometheus in pity brought us fire. Did Jupiter send him? Did he thank him? No. You know what he did. He seized our generous benefactor, bound him with massy chains to a desolate cliff, blasted him with thunderbolts, and stationed an immortal vulture to prey unscared forever and ever upon his wasteless vitals. That was a fair exponent of Jupiter's love for men.

Take modern heathenism. Its gods are numbered by the million, but none of them ever ask men to come and share their higher state. They don't want men in their abodes. Even if they did, who would wish to enter? Who could dwell with such horrid monstrosities as crowd the pantheons of India, Africa and the Feejee isles? The bare sight of their dead images, dragon-mouthed, serpent-girdled, gore-bespattered, haunts one for months with visions of horror. Their worshipers only fear them. They want no invitation to go to them, they only wish deliverance from their fiendish plagues.

And so you may go through the catalogue of all religions that now are or ever have been, and only in Christianity will you find a God who wants to draw men to himself, to bless them, to make them share his own eternal felicity. Now, is there not something very singular about this? Does it not show that in one thing, at least, and a most important thing, too, Christianity differs from all other religions? Does it not show that its God is infinitely above all other gods? that he alone is love — alone God?

But, my friend, there is another thing I want you to note. Singular as is this peculiarity of Christianity, there is another yet more singular. Did you ever notice that while the gospel sets before us a higher and more blessed heaven than any other religion, its hell is also deeper and darker than any other? That, my friend, is the wonderful thing. Not so much that Christianity says, "God is love," though compared with other religions this would be much; it is rather that right over against this declaration it affirms, "Our God is a consuming fire." What does that mean?

Think of it a moment. Did Zeus ever send men messengers to warn them of the judgments which would overtake them if they persisted in their sins? Did any heathen divinity ever do it? Where is the instance? Not one of them ever loved men enough to warn them of the fruits of sin. On the contrary, many of them are represented by their worshipers as seducing men into crime that they might have a pretext for tormenting them. How different the attitude of our God, standing with hands outstretched to even the most rebellious of the race, and crying, as only infinite tenderness can cry, "Turn ye, turn ye, for why will ye die?"

Look at the hells of your other religions. Pantheism has neither hell nor heaven. Denying personal immortality it necessarily denies both. Brahminism and Buddhism have no other hell than transmigration, and in that we are already. The old Zoroastrian hell was only a temporary purgatory, issuing in universal and everlasting blessedness. Classic heathenism had a Tartarus, but it was no hell. As a residence it was far preferable to some of the lower dens of sin in this world. Even the Old Testament is almost utterly silent on this dread theme. Christ is the first to plainly disclose to the world the awful reality. Possibly he was the first through whom God could make it known without repelling the race forever from him. In him love so offset divine justice that men could look upon its most appalling exhibition and adore.

I have heard of a strange class of people who claim that Jesus Christ was father and founder of the doctrine that there is no hell. You may have met such. They are scattered all through our Christian New England. Their only mistake is that Jesus Christ, instead of being the first denier of eternal punishment, was the first to teach it. Christ a denier that there is a hell! Let me read you a single passage from one of his discourses, just one consecutive paragraph.

"And if thy hand offend thee, cut it off; it is better for thee to enter into life maimed, than having two hands to go into hell, into the fire that never shall be quenched: where their worm dieth not, and the fire is not quenched. And if thy foot offend thee, cut it off: it is better for thee to enter halt into life, than having two feet to be cast into hell, into the fire that never shall be quenched: where their worm dieth not, and the fire is not quenched. And if thine eye offend thee, pluck it out: it is better for thee to enter into the kingdom of God with one eye, than having two eyes to be cast into hell fire: where their worm dieth not, and the fire is not quenched."*

Does that sound like a leaf from the gospel of John Murray? Take another of his solemn warnings. "Fear not them that kill the body and after that have no more that they can do. But I will forewarn you whom you shall fear. Fear him which after he hath killed, hath power to cast into hell, yea, I say unto you, fear him."

Is this the first, the original denier of an eternal hell? I need not tell you, who are students of ancient religions, that these people who attempt to father this denial upon Christ are wofully mistaken. Instead of being the first repudiator of eternal punishment, he was the first great religious teacher of the world, who ever clearly, unfalteringly, and authoritatively taught

* Mark ix. 43—48.

it. You may search through the sacred books of every nation anterior to Christ, and I challenge you to find in any of them such appalling language as that I have just read. Christ was the first to use it; and to this day no religious teacher has been able to state in stronger terms or to paint in darker shades the doom of a lost soul. The "outer darkness," the "weeping," the "gnashing of teeth," the "unquenchable fire," the "undying worm," the "binding," the "torments," the "devil and his angels," the interminable duration, all these dread elements and emblems of eternal perdition enter into Christ's own original picture of the final state of the impenitent.

But I wander. I was saying that the wonderful thing about Christianity is that it presents two such opposite peculiarities. Of all religions it alone sets before us a perfect heaven and a perfect hell. The mightiest imagination can never conceive a higher bliss or a deeper woe. Its invitations are the richest, but its warnings the dreadest ever brought home to the human mind. It is as peculiar in its awfulness as in its winningness. It excels all other religions as much in the one direction as in the other.

My friend, think a moment of this astonishing phenomenon. You are accustomed to philosophize on these things. What does it mean? There must be some reason for it. Can you explain it? Perhaps you would like to hear my explanation.

Well, my explanation is a very simple one. It is that Christianity is the one absolutely true religion. Other religions, containing only certain fragmentary elements of truth, are all included, swallowed up as it were, in the more comprehensive truth of Christianity? They have the conception of sin and of holiness, but their conception of sin can never go so deep, their conception of holiness can never rise so high as the Christian conception. Created by man's weak imagination, their gods can never be so strict as absolute justice, never so high as infinite love. Hence, Christianity at once underlies and overtops all other religions. What a proof is this that it is the only true religion!

Ah, yes! Good friend, connoisseur of religions, Christianity is true. In all its great foundation doctrines, you know it to be true. You know, for instance, that you have sinned against your Maker. You know you have no fellowship with him. The thought of standing before his judgment-seat fills you with alarm. There are times when in view of that great white throne you could wish you had never been born. And then when you think of your treatment of the blessed Saviour's invitation, you feel that God ought to withdraw his oft-grieved Spirit and cast you off forever. Oh! the burden that has sometimes rested upon your heart. What a realization of guilt and worthlessness! What self-reproach and condemnation!

What a fearful looking for of judgment and fiery indignation! How are the very localities of some of these experiences branded, as it were, into your inmost memory. As the lightning stroke sometimes leaves upon the human body pictures of adjacent objects, so these memorable flashes of God's convicting Spirit have photographed upon your very soul, as if for eternal preservation, the very spots where God sought you out only to be spurned. That village chapel, that woody nook, that midnight chamber, that lonely field where God said, Son, daughter, give me thine heart, and you refused,—you never can forget them. If lost, they will forever silence your every murmur against God. Oh, are not some of these convictions agitating your heart to-day? Is not the Spirit saying with me, "Come?" Oh, heed the call. Rouse from this fatal lethargy! Come to Jesus. By the mercies of God, I adjure you; by the love of Christ, by the patience of the Spirit, by the uncertainty of life, by the certainty of death, by the terrors of the judgment, by the bliss of the saved, by the woes of the lost, by every motive which can be drawn from heaven, or earth, or hell, come out from the doomed world of transgressors, and come to Jesus.

This is the first form of God's invitation to lost men. It is the call which seeks to wake the spiritually dead, and bids the sleeper rise.

But the Gospel has another "Come" a summons

for another class. We must not forget the secret seekers after God, who are found in almost every Christian congregation; souls not far from the kingdom, weary ones, who are sick of sin, who timorously sigh for a Saviour, saying, "Oh, that I knew where I might find him, that I might come even unto his seat." I fear we preachers too often overlook these precious ones over whom Christ's heart yearns so tenderly. You were afraid I was about to forget you, this time? No, no! I love too well to bring the Gospel invitation to such as you. Oh, it is such a different "Come" from that which is needed to awaken the slumbering sinner. Both are prompted by love, but this is so much gentler, tenderer, how can you hesitate to act upon it? Could any other invitation be so welcome to your burdened heart? Does he not offer all you sigh for? If you will but come to him and confess your sins, is he not faithful and just to forgive you your sins, and to cleanse you from all unrighteousness?

"Oh, yes," you say, "I believe it all; but somehow when it comes to the point of casting myself upon him as my perfect and everlasting Saviour, I lack the needed confidence and fall back."

That is it exactly. You lack confidence; in other words, faith. How are you going to get it? May I tell you how? If you cannot go, you can at least look to him. Behold him surrendering his pristine glory and assuming your lowly nature, that here in pain and sorrow he might work out your redemption. Is he not worthy of your confidence? Open another sense and listen, as in tones which have hushed the world he tells you his errand: "The Son of Man is come to seek and to save that which is lost." That means you; you know it does. Listen again, as he breathes over the ages the sweetest invitation of heaven: "Come unto me, all ye that labor and are heavy laden, and I will give you rest." That is what I call the second "Come" of the Gospel. It is Christ's "Come" to the penitent and broken-hearted. It is meant precisely for you. And to give you the greater confidence, he has said in words which shall live till time's last hour, "Him that cometh unto me I will in no wise cast out." Mark that pledge. Red-letter it in your Bibles. Inscribe it on the walls of your closet. "Him"—no matter who you are, young or old, rich or poor, black or white—"HIM THAT COMETH UNTO ME I WILL IN NO WISE CAST OUT." And lest you should not believe Christ, the prophet declares that in his day he was a "mighty Saviour." And lest you should not believe the prophet, the evangelist says that "to as many as received him, to them gave he power to become the sons of God." And lest you should not believe this evangelist, Paul declares that he was the chief of sinners, and yet that even he obtained mercy. And lest you should fail to believe Paul, Peter tells even the murderers of his Lord, "Whosoever shall call upon the name of the Lord shall be saved." And lest you should fail to believe Peter, John cries out, "The blood of Jesus Christ, his son, cleanseth us from all sin." And lest you should slight the testimony of former ages, the whole church militant rolls round the world the ceaseless confession:

> He breaks the power of canceled sin,
> He sets the prisoner free;
> His blood can make the foulest clean,
> His blood avails for me!

And, lest you should fail to believe the Church militant the Church triumphant chants in your very hearing, "Thou art worthy to take the book and to open the seals thereof; for thou wast slain and hast redeemed us to God by thy blood, out of every kindred and tongue and people and nation." And the number of these witnesses of Christ's saving power is ten thousand times ten thousand and thousands of thousands. And as they behold in heaven's light from what they were saved, and him who saved them, they shout with a loud voice, "Worthy is the Lamb that was slain to receive power and riches and wisdom and strength and honor and glory and blessing."

O timorous seeker, do you need any further testimony? Are you not ashamed in the face of such witnesses to doubt? Is not this High Priest able to save to the uttermost all who will come to God through him? O come then, and test his power, test his willingness, that then you may chime in with the chorus of earth and heaven. Do not tarry to make up any presentation robes or speeches. Come just as your predecessors have come. Come, timing your hasting footstep to the utterance:

> "Just as I am, without one plea,
> But that thy blood was shed for me,
> And that thou bid'st me come to thee,
> O Lamb of God, I come."

But the gospel has a third Come. It is Christ's call to the disciples. Do you remember how it runs? "If any man will come after me, let him deny himself and take up his cross and follow me." It is not a *coming to* a stationary Christ, but a *coming after* a forerunning one.

In a memorable battle of history an army of patriots were sore bestead. They were yielding their ground at every point. Vainly the captains shouted, "Forward." Vainly the colonels smote the retreating with their swords, yelled, "Back, ye cowards! Charge the foe!" Ever backward fell the staggering squadrons, until at length retreat was giving place to wildest rout and panic. Just at this critical moment, when all seemed lost, the commanding general flashed through their broken ranks, waving a sword which had never known dishonor, and shouting, "Follow *me*, boys!" At that word every nerve tingled, every pulse leaped, every heart bounded, every backward step was turned, and an invincible army charged under that leadership to victory.

That, brethren, is Christ's style of command. He never stands in the rear crying, "There's the enemy; up and at them!" O, no. The Captain of our salvation is a leader, and the hardest command he lays upon his soldiery is that oft-repeated "Follow me." No private in his army can ever complain that his general exposes him more than he does himself. What a blessed and cheering thought is this. How it inspires the weary and fainting. How it stops the mouth of complaint, and makes petulance ashamed of itself. O, disconsolate brother! Does your way seem rough and thorny? Your Lord has trodden it with bleeding feet before you. Does his service necessitate great sacrifice? It may be, but tell me, is it equal to his sacrifice for you, who though he was rich yet for your sake became poor, that you through his poverty might be rich? Have you for his sake surrendered such riches, or welcomed such poverty? You find his commandments hard, do you? Mention one which he did not himself obey before laying it upon you. Is much prayer irksome? How many whole nights have you spent praying in lonely mountains apart? Is fasting grievous to the flesh? When did you try it for forty days and forty nights in succession? O! I love to march under such a leader, one who never says, "Go" on, but always "Come" on.

Yes, brethren, we are soldiers. We are on hostile soil. But when I survey my own soldiering for Christ, and that of most of my comrades, I am astonished that with such an army he has ever won a single skirmish. What blundering, what sloth, what mutinies, have characterized our service! How many of our number have been play soldiers, delighted, it may be, with the evolutions of the drill-room, but always stacking arms at the close of the exercise with no thought of resuming them again until the next appointed drill. Do you recognize the class? These are they who are always found with clock-like regularity at church and in the social meeting, who are perchance foremost in prayer and exhortation, but who can go home and work all the week with a swearing neighbor without ever venturing to rebuke his sin or invite him to Christ. Then how many on the other hand neglect and trample on Christ's army discipline, in a fanatical zeal to do more fighting. These you all know. They are the men and women, who without self-restraint, or system, or consistent piety, are always pitching into everybody and everything, anxious only for a fight. Many of them mean well, and at first dash forth to battle more brilliantly than the regulars, but when the long marches and steady actions come on, when vigils and fastings, and sleeping upon arms become necessary, Oh, how worse than useless, how demoralizing they are. Again how many forget both discipline and fighting, and not only impede the movements of the army, but also dampen its ardor and destroy its *esprit*. These are the backsliders, the greatest of all curses to the army of Christ. Were they only open mutineers or deserters, they could at least be shot. That would at once relieve the service of their cumbrance and heighten the discipline of the body. But these cowardly, moping, stupid laggards, who neither love their general nor hate the foe, to what earthly purpose can they be put? I wonder not that Christ has said of them, "They are henceforth good for nothing but to be cast out and to be trodden under foot of men." Then again how many whole divisions of the army have wavered, revolted, and gone over to the enemy. How many more are fighting amongst themselves just because of a different banner or uniform. How few are the good soldiers, the undemoralized regiments, the victorious divisions!

But let us not be disheartened. There never was less reason for being so. Our leader can never be defeated. Each season is chronicling stupendous victories. The last great heathen powers are crumbling, and the outposts of Christ's kingdom already encircle the world. With each new victory the spirit of the army rises. Many of the lukewarm are catching inspiration, many of the faint-hearted are waxing valiant, many of the quarrelsome are making peace, many of the divided, union. Long stationary regiments are wheeling into line, long-lost divisions are coming into view. The whole magnificent array, many-tinted, many-tongued, is getting into action. Immanuel's "Come" echoes from the far front to farthest rear. All burn to share in the common victory. Thank God it is so. God speed each separate company and corps!

But I hear a voice, feeble and broken, and it asks, "Is there not one other Come, for such as I? I once heard the first Come, and the second. I obeyed. I came to the blessed Jesus, and since that time I have been coming after him. I have loved to hear his voice in the van, and to fight under his banner. I have been his soldier these thirty, forty, fifty years. But now I am old and feeble. My eyes are dim, and I halt upon my staff. I can no more go forth to battle. Is there no different Come for me?"

Oh, yes, aged comrade. Or ever you are aware, a new, delightful call shall reach you, a voice from heaven, saying, "Come up higher." And these ears, now dull of hearing, shall be unstopped, and ravishing music shall flow in. These fading eyes shall be relighted, and you shall see angels waiting to translate you to your Lord. Oh, to come thus convoyed into his presence! Oh, to see him face to face! And before you half explore that wondrous Paradise, there'll be another coming, grander than ever angel dreamed. And they shall come from the east and from the west, and from the north and from the south. And all nations shall be gathered together. And the great white throne shall be set up and Christ shall sit upon it. And he shall separate them one from another, even as a shepherd divideth his sheep from the goats. Then, white-haired brother, then shalt thou hear the final "Come" of history. Oh, what joy will there be upon the right hand. How lustrous will beam those angel faces! What light will fill the eyes of ancient king and prophet—eyes that longed to see Christ's day, but died without the sight. What exultation will swell the heart of holy martyrs and apostles. Yea, what sweet suspenseful blessedness shall fill and sway and agitate thy heart, my time-bowed brother, as there, replenished with immortal youth, star-crowned and robed and palmed, thou, too, shalt wait with all the saints that final, promised utterance. And when at length over that hushed sea of being the voice of the King shall send forth his last concluding invitation, that concluding invitation shall be like the first: "Come! Come, ye blessed of my Father, inherit the kingdom prepared for you from the foundation of the world!"

Such, my brethren, is the outcome of this gospel invitation. Redemption from all sorrow and all sin, likeness to the white and holy Christ, eternal life with God in heaven. To this we call you to-day. The Spirit and the Bride say, Come. Oh ye that hear, say

Come. Oh, ye that are in any wise athirst, come. And whosoever will, let him take this water of life freely. Blessed word, "whosoever will." As one has said, that "whosoever" is the great bell of God's eternal and impartial love. It rings all home alike. Its mighty boom of promise drowns each doubt and cavil.

Come, thou swearer; come, thou that hast trifled with gracious convictions; come, backslider; come, thou that hast deemed thyself a reprobate; come, thou that fearest to have quenched the Spirit evermore: "whosoever," "whosoever will, let him take of the water of life freely."

# FINAL PERMANENCE OF MORAL CHARACTER.

## A MONDAY LECTURE.

BY

REV. JOSEPH COOK.

# FINAL PERMANENCE OF MORAL CHARACTER.

### BY REV. JOSEPH COOK.

WHEN Charles IX. of France was importuned to kill Coligny, he for a long time refused to do so publicly or secretly, but at last he gave way, and consented in these memorable words: "Assassinate Admiral Coligny, but leave not a Huguenot alive in France to reproach me." So came the massacre of St. Bartholomew. When the soul resolves to assassinate some holy motive; when the spirit determines to kill, in the inner realm, Admiral Coligny, it, too, delays for a while, and when it gives way usually says: "Assassinate this accuser of mine, but leave not an accusing accomplice of his in all my kingdom alive to reproach me." So comes the massacre of the desire to be holy.

Emerson quotes the Welsh Triad as saying: "God himself cannot procure good to the wicked." Julius Muller, Dorner, Rothe, Schleiermacher, no less than Plato, Aristotle, and Socrates, assert that in the nature of things there *can* be no blessedness without holiness. Confucius said: "Heaven means principle."

But what if a soul permanently *loses* principle? *Si vis fugere a Deo fuge ad Deum,* is the Latin proverb. If you wish to flee from God, flee to him. The soul cannot escape from God; and can two walk together unless they are agreed? Surely there are a few certainties in religion, or several points clear to exact ethical science in relation to the natural conditions of the peace of the soul.

It is plainly possible that a man may fall into free permanent dissimilarity of feeling with God, or fail to attain a predominant desire to be holy.

If he does this, it remains scientifically certain that even omnipotence and omniscience cannot force upon such a character, blessedness. There can be no blessedness without holiness; and there can be no holiness without a supreme love of what God loves, and a supreme hate of what God hates. It is possible that a man may so disarrange his nature as not to attain a permanent and predominant desire to be holy.

Theodore Parker, as his biographers admit, must be called a great reader rather than a great scholar. But, De Wette, his German master, although most of his works have ceased to be authorities in Biblical research, ought to have prevented Theodore Parker from asserting that the Founder of Christianity did not teach that there may be a failure in a free agent to attain a permanent and predominant desire to be holy. Theodore Parker himself ought to have

# Final Permanence of Moral Character. 265

prevented himself from that assertion. In his earlier career, he held that Our Lord did teach a possibility of the failure of some forever and forever to attain a supreme love of what God loves, and a supreme hate of what God hates. He thought that the New Testament, properly interpreted, does contain in it a statement that it is possible for a man to fail permanently to attain the predominant desire to be holy, and this was one of Parker's reasons for rejecting the authority of the New Testament. But toward the end of his career he tried to persuade Frances Power Cobbe that the Founder of Christianity did not teach that any will be lost. Parker's writings are self-contradictory on this supreme topic, most of the real difficulties of which he skipped.

It is the wisdom of all science, however, never to skip difficulties. I know how widely intellectual unrest on the topic I am now introducing fills minds that never have been much troubled by Theodore Parker. I know that many conscientious and learned persons have asked themselves the question the disciples once asked Our Lord: "Are there few that be saved?" He answered that inquiry very distinctly: "Yes, there are few." Does science answer in the same way?

It would not follow, my friends, even if you were to take Our Lord's answer as supreme authority, as I do, that this universe is a failure. All ages to come are to be kept in view; all other worlds. Our

Lord's words referred to our present evil generation; and, if you ask the central question in the best modern form, you must answer it in his way. How many, in the present state of our earth, love predominantly what God loves, and hate predominantly what God hates? How many have acquired predominant similarity of feeling with God? Only those who have, can be at peace in his presence, either here or hereafter. That is as certain as any deduction from our intuitions concerning the nature of things. As sure as that a thing cannot be and not be at the same time in the same sense, so sure is it, that a man cannot be at peace with God when he loves what he hates and hates what he loves. There must be harmony or dissonance between them, and dissonance is its own punishment. Dissimilarity of feeling with God carries with it immense wages, in the nature of things. In the name of science, ask, Are there few that have acquired a predominant love of what God loves and a predominant hate of what God hates? We must answer in the name of science, that broad is the way and wide is the gate, which, in our evil generation, leads to dissimilarity of feeling with God, and many there be who go in thereat; but strait is the way and narrow is the gate which leads to similarity of feeling with God, and few are they in our time that find it. But there are other worlds; there are other ages. "Save yourselves from this untoward generation."

Who knows that in the final summing up the number of the lost may be greater than that of the saved? or, as Lyman Beecher used to say in this city, "greater than the number of our criminals in penal institutions is in contrast with the whole of the population." But I talk of the galaxies; I talk of the infinities, and of the eternities; and not merely of this world, in which you and I are to work out our deliverance from the love of sin, and the guilt of sin, and have reason to do so with fear and trembling.

I ask no man here to-day, or any day, to take my opinions. You are requested to notice whether discussion is clear; not whether it is orthodox. Let us put aside entirely all ecclesiastical and denominational tests. This Lectureship has for its purpose simply the discussion of the clear, the true, the new and the strategic in the relations between science and religion.

What are some of the more important natural laws which enable us to estimate scientifically the possible extent of the natural penalties of sin?

I. *Under irreversible natural law, sin produces judicial blindness.*

Kill Admiral Coligny, drive out the Huguenots, permit the massacre of St. Bartholomew, and you have made a new France. Carlyle says that it pleased France to slit her own veins and let out the best blood she had, and that she did this on the night of the massacre of St. Bartholomew; and that after that she was historically another creature. Having killed Coligny you cannot look his friends in the face; you kill them and your kingdom is a new one. When a man sins against light, there comes upon him an unwillingness to look upon the accusing illumination, and the consequence is that he turns away from it. But that effect itself becomes a cause. Keep your eyes upon your Shakespeare, upon your Greek poets, or upon whatever is a good mirror of human nature, and tell me whether these six propositions are not all scientifically demonstrable:—

1. Truth possessed but not obeyed becomes unwelcome.

2. It is therefore shut out of the voluntary activities of memory and reflection, as it gives pain.

3. The passions it should check grow therefore stronger.

4. The moral emotions it should feed grow weaker.

5. An ill-balanced state of the soul thus arises and tends to become habitual.

6. That ill-balanced state renders the soul blind to the truths most needed to rectify its condition.

"On the temperate man," says Aristotle,* "are attendant, perhaps forthwith, by motion of his temperance, good opinions and appetites as to pleasures; but on the intemperate, the opposite."

* Rhetoric, Bohn's Ed., p. 70.

A man sins against light boldly. To the divine "I ought" he answers, "I will not;" to the divine "thou shalt" or "thou oughtest" he replies, "I will not." The consequence instantly is that he ceases to be at peace with himself; and light, instead of becoming a blessing, is to him an accusation. The slant javelin of truth that was intended to penetrate him with rapture, fills him now with torture. If we give ourselves to an exact study of the soul's pains and pleasures, there is in man no greater bliss than conscience can afford, and no greater pain than it can inflict. In this stage of existence the highest bliss comes from similarity of feeling with God, and the highest pain from dissimilarity of feeling with him. The greatest pains and pleasures, therefore, are set over against our greatest duties, and so God's desire that we should agree with him is shown by our living under the points of all these penalties and blisses. But light having become an accuser, man turns away from it. Then the virtues which that light ought to quicken are allowed to languish. The vices which that light ought to repress grow more vigorous. Repeated acts of sin result in a continued state of dissimilarity of feeling with God. That state is an effect, but it becomes a cause. According to New England theology, sin exists only in acts of choice; but the newest school of that theology need have no war with the oldest, for the former recognizes as fully as the latter can, that the state of dissimilarity of feeling with God is the source of the evil acts of choice. That state of the dispositions is the copious fountain of sin, and as such is properly called depravity. This state, continuing, becomes a habit; then that habit, continuing long, becomes chronic, and so the result is an ill-balanced growth of the character.

When I hung my hammock up last summer on the shores of Lake George, I noticed that the trees nearest the light at the edge of the forest had larger branches than those in the interior of the wood; and that the same tree would throw out a long branch toward the light and a short one toward obscurity in the interior of the forest. Just so a man grows toward the light to which he turns. According to the direction in which he turns with his supreme affection he grows; and, as he grows, he balances; and, under the irreversible natural law of moral gravitation, — as fixed, as scientific a certainty in the universe as the law of physical gravitation, — as he balances so he falls; and, according to science, after a tree has fallen under that law, the prostrate trunk continues to be under the law, and, therefore, as it falls so it lies.

Under moral gravitation no less surely than under physical, every free object that falls out of the sky strikes on its heavier side. They showed me at Amherst the other day a meteorite that dropped out of the azure, and it struck on which side? Of course on its heavier. As the stream runs, so it wears its channel; as it wears its channel, so it runs. All the mythologies of the globe recognize this fearful law of judicial blindness.

Go yonder into Greenland with Dr. Ranke, and you will find a story among the men of the lonely North to the effect that if a sorcerer will make a stirrup out of a strip of seal skin and wind it around his limbs, three times about his heart, and thrice about his neck, and seven times about his forehead, and then knot it before his eyes, that sorcerer, when the lamps are put out at night, may rise into space and fly whithersoever his leading passion dictates. So we put ourselves into the stirrup of predominant love of what God hates, and predominant hate of what God loves, and we coil the strands about our souls. They are thrice wound about our heart, three times around the neck, seven times around our foreheads, and knotted before our eyes. If the poor savages yonder, where the stars look down four months of the year without interruption, are right in their sublime theory as to the solemnities of the universe, we, too, when the lamps are out, shall rise into the Unseen Holy and fly whithersoever our leading passion dictates.

Greenland says that hunters once went out and found a revolving mountain, and that, attempting to cross the chasm between it and the firm land, some of these men were crushed as the mountain revolved.

But they finally noticed that the gnarled, wheeling mass had a red side and a white side. They waited till the white side came opposite them; and then, ascending the mountain, found that a king lived on its summit; made themselves loyal to him; surrendered themselves to him, affectionately and irreversibly; and afterwards found themselves able to go and come safely. But the mountain had a red side, and it turned and turned, and there was no safety on it except on the white side and in loyalty to the king at the summit in the clouds. That mythology of the North, lately read for us by scholars, has in it eternal verity and a kind of solemnity like that of the long shining of the Arctic stars, and the tumbling icebergs, and the peaceable gurgle of the slow-heaving Polar Ocean, far-gleaming under the boreal lights or the midnight Arctic sun. Stunted, you think the men of that zone? Why, on the banks of the Charles yonder, your Longfellow, taking up a German poet, finds the same idea in far less sublime and subtle imagery, and translates it for its majesty and truth:

> "The mills of God grind slowly,
> But they grind exceeding small."

To me there is in Macbeth nothing so terrible as Lady Macbeth's invocation of the spirits which produce moral callousness in the soul. There is no passage in that sublime treatise on conscience which we call Macbeth, so sublime to me as this, on the law of judicial blindness:

> The raven himself is hoarse
> That croaks the fatal entrance of Duncan
> Under my battlements. Come, you spirits,
> .... Unsex me here
> And fill me from the crown to the toe top-full
> Of direst cruelty! Make thick my blood.
> Stop up the access and passage to remorse.
> .... Come, thick Night,
> And pall thee in the dunnest smoke of hell,
> That my keen knife see not the wound it makes,
> Nor heaven peep through the blanket of the dark,
> To cry "Hold! Hold!"
> (Macbeth, Act i., Scene 5.)

That invocation is likely to be uttered by every soul which has said "I will not" to the divine "I ought." It is as sure to be answered as natural law is to be irreversible. Macbeth himself, in a similar mood, says:

> Come, seeling night,
> Scarf up the tender eye of pitiful day.
> Cancel and tear to pieces that great bond
> Which keeps me pale. Light thickens, and the crow
> Makes wing to the rooky wood.
> (Macbeth, Act iii., Scene 2.)

Have you ever offered in the rooky wood of sorcerous temptation, a prayer for blindness? *In the nature of things every sin against light draws blood on the spiritual retina.*

You say that after death you are to have more illumination, and that therefore you will reform beyond the grave! How do you know that you will see greater illumination, even if you are in the presence of it? How do you know that you will love it even if you do see it? There can be no blessedness without holiness; there can be no holiness without a free, affectionate acknowledgment of God as King, or a supreme love of what he loves and hate of what he hates. Are you likely to obtain these soon under the law of judicial blindness? You will have what you like; but do you like the light? You have more and more illumination now as the years pass! Do you see it? Do you love it? There are two questions about this greater light beyond the grave: first, will you see it? second, will you like it? Unless you have authority in the name of science for answering both these questions in the affirmative, you have no right in the name of science to rely on a mere possibility, on a guess, and take your leap into the Unseen, depending on a riddle. I, for one, will not do this for myself; and I will not teach others to do so.

Shakespeare has not left us in doubt at all on this theme, for in another place he says:

> But when we in our viciousness grow hard,
> .... the wise gods seal our eyes;
> In our own slime drop our clear judgments, make us
> Adore our errors: laugh at us, while we strut
> To our confusion.
> —Antony and Cleopatra, Act iii., Scene 11.

Carlyle quotes out of the Koran a story of the dwellers by the Dead Sea, to whom Moses was sent.

They sniffed and sneered at Moses; saw no comeliness in Moses; and so he withdrew, but Nature and her rigorous veracities did not withdraw. When next we find the dwellers by the Dead Sea, they, according to the Koran, were all changed into apes. "By not using their souls they lost them." "And now," continues Carlyle, "their only employment is to sit there and look out into the smokiest, dreariest, most undecipherable sort of universe; only once in seven days they do remember that they once had souls. Hast thou never, O traveler, fallen in with parties of this tribe? Methinks they have grown somewhat numerous in our day."

The old Greek proverb was, that the avenging deities are shod with wool; but the wool grows on the eyelids that refuse the light. "Whom the gods would destroy they first make mad;" but the insanity arises from judicial blindness.

Jeremy Taylor says that whoever sins against light kisses the lips of a blazing cannon.

I never saw a dare-devil face that had not in it something of both the sneak and the fool. The sorcery of sin is that it changes a man into a sneak and a fool, but the fool does not know that he is a sneak, and the sneak does not know that he is a fool. If I were a sculptor I would represent sin with two faces, like those of Janus, looking in opposite directions; one should be idiotic, the other Machiavellian.

But the one face could not see the other. The idiot would not know that he is Machiavellian; the Machiavelli would not know that he is idiotic. The sneak would not know that he is a fool, nor the fool that he is a sneak.

II. *Under irreversible natural law there is a self-propagating power in sin.*

Of course this self-propagating power depends upon the law of judicial blindness very largely, but by no means exclusively. So are we made that every effect in the growth of our characters becomes a cause, and every good effect no less than every bad one.

The laws of the self-propagating power of habit bless the righteous as much as they curse the wicked. The laws by which we attain supreme bliss are the laws by which we descend to supreme woe. In the ladder up and the ladder down in the universe, the rungs are in the same side-pieces. The self-propagating power of sin and the self-propagating power of holiness are one law. The law of judicial blindness is one with that by which the pure in heart see God, and they who walk toward the east find the morning brighter and brighter to the perfect day.

Of course, I shall offend many if I assert that there may be penalty that has no remedial tendency. But, gentlemen, I ask you to be clear, and to remember that an unwelcome truth is really not destroyed by shutting the eyes to it. There are three kinds of natural laws, the physical, the organic, and the moral. *I affirm that "Never too late to mend" is not a doctrine of science in the domain of the physical laws, nor is it in that of the organic.*

Under the physical laws of gravitation a ship may careen to the right or left and only a remedial effect be produced. The danger may teach the crew seamanship; it makes men bold and wise. Thus the penalty of violating up to a certain point the physical law is remedial in its tendency. But, let the ship careen beyond a certain line and it capsizes. If it be of iron it remains at the bottom of the sea, and hundreds and hundreds of years of suffering of that penalty has no tendency to bring it back. Under the physical natural laws, plainly there is such a thing as its being too late to mend. In their immeasurable domain there is a distinction between penalty that has a remedial tendency, and penalty that has no remedial tendency at all.

So, under the organic law, your tropical tree, gashed at a certain point, may throw forth its gums, and even have greater strength than before; but gashed beyond the centre, cut through, the organic law is so far violated that the tree falls; and after a thousand years, you do not expect to see the tree escape from the dominion of the law which is enforcing upon it penalty, do you? There is no tendency in that penalty toward remedial effect; none at all; and you know it. Therefore, under the organic laws there is such a thing as its being too late to mend.

Now, gentlemen, keep your eyes fastened upon the great principle of analogy, which Newton and Butler call the supreme rule in science, and ask yourselves whether, if you were to find some strange animal in a geological stratum, and if you were to know, by having one of its hands free, that it had three fingers, and if you were to find two fingers on the other hand free from the rock, and both shutting toward the palm, you would not infer that the third finger, if you could loosen it from the rock, would also be found closing toward the palm? Just so I ask whether, if we find that under two sets of natural laws which are all included under three classes, there is incontrovertibly such a thing as penalty without remedial effect, there may not be the same under the third set? Two fingers shut toward the palm. I cannot quite trace the whole range of the moral law; but I know by analogy that, if two fingers shut toward the palm, the third probably does. *If there is such a thing as its being forever too late to mend under the organic and the physical natural law, probably, and more than probably, there is such a thing under the moral natural law.*

Yes; but you say the will is free, and, therefore, that it cannot be supposed that a man will fall into final dissimilarity of feeling with God; or can so lose the desire to be holy, that he will not choose the right when greater light comes. You affirm that the self-propagating power of sin may place necessity upon the disordered nature. You say that the denial that all moral penalty is remedial requires us to deny that the will of lost souls continues free. I beg your pardon again, and that in the name of science. Gentlemen, there may be certainty where there is no necessity.

Is John Milton putting together a self-contradiction when he pictures Satan as making evil his good, and as yet retaining a free will? Is he uttering self-contradiction when he shows us a fiendish character which retains yet some elements of its original brightness? Has Milton's Satan lost free will?

Origen used to teach that the prince of fiends might return to a glad allegiance to God; and so did Robert Burns, whom Emerson commends for using these words, originally written to attack the proposition I am now defending, but, after all, containing most subtle confirmation of it:

> "auld Nickie-ben!
> An' wad ye tak a thought and men',
> Ye aiblins might—I dinna ken—
> Still hae a stake."

No, gentlemen; the self-propagating power of sin may produce a state of soul in which evil is chosen as good, and in which it is forever too late to mend, and yet not destroy free will.

I affirm that you know that John Milton's Satan is not an impossible character. You say you do not care what Milton says; but I am not asking you to take his theology. Let me not be misunderstood in my citations of the poets as witnesses to what man is. Paradise Lost is a great classic, and no poem attains that rank if it is full of manifest absurdities. Now, Milton's Satan is a character in which the disarrangement of the soul is supposed to have become permanent; he has fallen into final permanence of evil character; and yet he is represented as absolutely free — and not very near annihilation! Burns says if Satan had the predominant wish to do so, he might mend. I appeal to classical literature to show that a permanent evil character, with a free will, is not a psychological self-contradiction. You admit this readily, age after age, in your great classics; but the instant I, here, standing face to face with natural religion, assert that there may be a final permanence of free character, bad as well as good, and good as well as bad, you stand aghast at your own proceeding. Gentlemen, you and I must have no cross purposes with the nature of things. If Milton's description is not a psychological self-contradiction, there may be a person of permanently bad character, absolutely free and therefore responsible.

III. *Under irreversible natural law, character tends to a final permanence, good or bad. In the nature of the case, a final permanence is attained but once.*

If asked whether final permanence of character is a natural law, what should you say, if we were to speak without reference to conclusions in religious science? How have men in all ages expressed themselves in literature and philosophy on this theme? Is it not perfectly certain that all the great writers of the world justify the proposition that character tends to a final permanence, good or bad?

Gentlemen, this universe up to the edge of the tomb is not a joke. There are in this life serious differences between the right hand and the left. Nevertheless, in our present career, a man has but one chance. Even if you come weighted into the world, as Sinbad was with the Old Man of the Mountain, you have but one chance. Time does not fly in a circle, but forth and right on. The wandering, squandering, desiccated moral leper is gifted with no second set of early years. There is no fountain in Florida that gives perpetual youth, and the universe might be searched, probably, in vain for such a spring. Waste your youth; you shall have but one chance. Waste your middle life; you shall have but one chance. Waste your old age; you shall have but one chance. It is an irreversible natural law that character attains final permanence, and in the nature of things final permanence can come but once. This world is fearfully and wonderfully made, and so are we, and we shall escape neither ourselves nor these stupendous laws. It is not to me a pleasant thing to exhibit these truths from the side of terror; but, on the other side, these are the truths of bliss; for by this very law through which all character tends to become unchanging, a soul that attains a final permanence of good character runs but one risk and is delivered once for all from its torture and unrest. It has passed the bourne from behind which no man is caught out of the fold. He who is the force behind all natural law, is the keeper of his sheep, and no one is able to pluck them out of his hand. Himself without variableness or shadow of turning, he maintains the irreversibleness of all natural forces, one of which is the insufferably majestic law by which character tends to assume final permanence, good as well as bad.

IV. *Under irreversible natural law there may be in the soul a permanent failure to attain a predominant and enduring desire to be holy.*

Go to India; open the Bhagvat Gheta, a Hindoo book your Emerson greatly reveres; look into the subtlest thought of the Hindoo philosophy and you will find these two searching sentences, which are all I need in reply to any criticisms I have heard:

1. "Repeated sin impairs the judgment."

2. "He whose judgment is impaired sins repeatedly."*

With equal scientific clearness Julius Müller says: "*Such is the constitution of things that unwillingness to goodness may ripen into eternal voluntary opposition to it.*" † By irreversible natural law all character tends to a final permanence, good or bad. In the nature of things a final permanence can come but once.

The inveteracy of sin! Have you ever heard of that? Out of its acknowledged inveteracy will *not* easily arise its evanescence. Out of its prolongation comes its inveteracy, and out of its inveteracy may come its permanence.

Here and now I do not touch the topic of the annihilation of those who fall into permanent dissimilarity of feeling with God, for I do not see that this cause produces any tendency to annihilation in this world, when a man becomes incorrigibly bad. Villains do not commonly lack force. Your Nero, with his murders and leprosies, has put his nature out of order; but look at his evil face, in marble, on the Capitoline hill, and you start as if gazing into a demon's eyes. He is as little weak as a volcano. What do men mean when they talk of vice annihilating

---

* Prof. Monier Williams, Indian Wisdom, Cambridge, England, 1876.
† Doct. of Sin, vol. ii.

souls? It disarranges them, but disarrangement is not annihilation. Tacitus says that Nero heard the sound of a trumpet and the groans from the grave of his mother, Agrippina, whom he had murdered. His disarrangement was not derangement. Acting fitfully, all the wheels of the faculties continued to exist in Nero, and they are none of them without movement. They grind on each other, no doubt, but I do not find that spiritual wheels can be pulverized. Do you know how they can be? This idea that evil is to annihilate us ought to have some distinct scientific support in the experience of this life.

In the Singalese books of Gotama, Buddha, written under the shadow of the Himalayas, we find the statement that "as surely as the pebble cast heavenward abides not there, but returns to the earth, so, proportionate to thy deed, good or ill, will the desire of thy heart be meted out to thee, in whatever form or world thou shalt enter." It was the opinion of Socrates, recorded with favor by Plato, that "the wicked would be too well off if their evil deeds came to an end." * All disloyalty to the still small voice which declares what ought to be, is followed by pain. *What if it were not?* Is God God, if, with unscientific liberalism, we in our philosophy put the throne of the universe upon rockers, and make of it an easy-chair from which lullabys are sung, both to the evil and to the good?

* Jowett's Plato, Introduction to Phædo.

"Whatever we do, God is on our side." So say many who would not dare to affirm that, whatever we do, the nature of things is on our side. But the nature of things is only the total outcome of the requirements of the perfections of the divine nature. God is behind the nature of things, and you and I cannot trifle with him any more than with it. He was, he is, he is to come. It was, it is, it is to come. It is he.

Great literature always recognizes the law of moral gravitation. Seeking the deepest modern words, I open, for instance, Thomas Carlyle, and read:

"'Penalties:' Quarrel not with the old phraseology, good reader; attend rather to the thing it means. The word was heard of old, with a right solemn meaning attached to it, from theological pulpits and such places; and may still be heard there, with a half meaning, or with no meaning, though it has become rather obsolete to modern ears. But the *thing* should not have fallen obsolete; the thing is a grand and solemn truth, expressive of a silent law of Heaven, which continues forever valid. The most untheological of men may still assert the thing; and invite all men to notice it, as a silent monition and prophecy in this universe; to take it, with more of awe than they are wont, as a correct reading of the will of the Eternal in respect of such matters, and in their modern sphere, to bear the same well in mind.

"The want of loyalty to the Maker of this universe —he who wants that, what else has he or can he have? If you do not, you man or you nation, love the truth enough, but try to make a chapman-bargain with truth, instead of giving yourself wholly, soul and body and life, to her, truth will not live with you, truth will depart from you; and only logic, 'wit' (for example, 'London Wit'), sophistry, virtu, the æsthetic arts, and perhaps (for a short while) bookkeeping by double entry, will abide with you. You will follow falsity, and think it truth, you unfortunate man or nation. You will, right surely, you for one, stumble to the devil; and are every day and hour, little as you imagine it, making progress thither."\*

This majestic key-note of scientific, ethical truth is the deep tone that leads the anthem of all great thought since the world began. Open now Theodore Parker, and how harshly his words clash with Carlyle's: "The infinite perfection of God is the cornerstone of all my theological and religious teaching; the foundation, perhaps, of all that is peculiar in my system. It is not known to the Old Testament or the New; it has never been accepted by any sect in the Christian world. The idea of God's imperfection has been carried out with dreadful logic in the Christian scheme. In the ecclesiastical conception of the Deity there is a fourth person in the Godhead,—namely, the

\* Carlyle, Frederick the Great, vol. i., pp. 270, 271.

Devil, — an outlying member, unacknowledged, indeed, the complex of all evil, but as much a part of Deity as either Son or Holy Ghost, and far more powerful than all the rest, who seem but jackals to provide for this roaring lion." *

What is in the lines here in Parker is not so painful as what is between the lines. "God is a perfect creator," writes Parker, "making all from a perfect motive, for a perfect purpose. The motive must be love; the purpose welfare. The perfect creator is a perfect providence; love becoming a universe of perfect welfare." †

"Optimism is the religion of science." "*Every fall is a fall upwards.*" ‡

*One feels in reading Theodore Parker, that whatever we do God is on our side. Carlyle is of a very different opinion,* and is moved by no faith deeper than that the distinction between duty and its opposite is "quite infinite." Place side by side this free-thinker, Carlyle, and that free-thinker, Parker, and ask which is the truer of the two to the deep intuitions of the soul? Contrast the seriousness of Buddha and the tone of this man of Massachusetts Bay! Compare Socrates and Plato under the shade of the Acropolis with this modern man under the shade of what? Of a stunted mental philosophy; rooted well,

---

\* Weiss, Life of Parker, vol. i., p. 470.
† Ibid., p. 471.   ‡ Theism, pp. 408–417.

indeed, in our soil at his time, but only a very imperfect growth as yet; and hardly risen above the ground when the attempt was made here to deny the existence of sin and of its natural wages in the universe in the name of an intuitive philosophy, which asserts precisely the opposite in both cases.

The self-propagating power of habit, acting in the sphere of the holy affections, places the nature of things on the side of righteousness.

The same self-propagating power of habit, acting in the sphere of evil affections, arranges the nature of things against evil.

Good has but one enemy, the evil; but the evil has two enemies, the good and itself.*

Judicial blindness increases the self-propagating power of evil; remunerative vision increases the self-propagating power of holiness.

"Every man," says the Spanish proverb, "is the son of his own deeds." "Every action," says Richter, "becomes more certainly an eternal mother than it is an eternal daughter." † These are the irreversible laws according to which all character tends to final permanence, good or bad.

V. *Under irreversible natural law there may exist in the universe eternal sin.*

It is not my duty here, as it is on the Sabbaths, to

---

\* See Julius Müller, Doctrine of Sin, vol. ii.
† Titan, vol. i., cycle 105.

expound the scriptures, but you will allow me to say that "eternal sin" is a scriptural phrase. As all these scholars know, we must read in the twenty-ninth verse of the third chapter of Mark, *hamartematos*, and not *kriseos*. He who sinneth against the Holy Ghost is in danger of "eternal sin."

Theodore Parker used to say that the profoundest expressions in the New Testament are those which are most likely to have been correctly reported. What phrase on this theme is profounder than "eternal sin?" Dean Alford well says that "it is to the critical treatment of the sacred text that we owe the restoration of such important and deep-reaching expressions as this." Lange calls it "a strong and pregnant expression."

It is not the best way in which to teach the truth of future punishment to say that a man is punished forever and forever for the sins of that hand's breadth of duration we call time. If the soul does not repent of these with contrition, and not merely with attrition, the nature of things forbids its peace. But the Biblical and the natural truth is, that prolonged dissimilarity of feeling with God may end in eternal sin. If there is eternal sin, there will be eternal punishment. Final permanence of character, under the laws of judicial blindness and the self-propagating power of sin, is the truth emphasized by both God's word and his works.

s

VI. *While sin continues, God cannot forgive it without making the sinner worse.*

In this city, six thousand people were told the other evening, with great depth of thought, that if a child deliberately lies, and you forgive the child, before he has exhibited any sorrow for the act, you make the child worse. That is, indeed, a very simple instance of the moral law, but in scientific minds there is no doubt that the moral law is equally universal with the physical. If you will measure a little arc of the physical law, you can measure the whole circle.

If I were to take a flight into space, I should not run beyond the knowledge that I have acquired here of the law of gravitation. That law is one in all worlds, so far as science knows. So, too, if I understand the properties of light here, I understand them in Orion and the Pleiades. A good terrestrial text-book on light or gravitation would be of service in the North Star. The universality and the unity of law make our earth, although but an atom, immensity itself in its revelations of truth.* Now, if I know that a man has deliberately lied to me, I cannot here under the moral law forgive him before he repents without making him worse. If I know that, then there is reason to believe that God cannot, in the nature of things, forgive a free agent that has incurred personal demerit by the choice

* See Dana, Geology, chap. I.

of wrong motives, till he has repented, without making that agent worse. The nature of things, gentlemen, it is the same yesterday, to-day, and forever.

Here is a Boston sonnet, entitled "A Far Shore," and it asserts the universality of the moral law, as well as of the physical and the organic, and so it applies not only to Greece and Italy and the shadow of the Pyramids, but also to that undiscovered country from whose bourne no traveler returns:

> On a far shore my land swam far from sight,
>   But I could see familiar native stars;
>   My home was shut from me by ocean bars,
> Yet home hung there above me in the night;
> Unchanged fell down on me Orion's light;
>   As always, Venus rose, and fiery Mars;
>   My own the Pleiads yet, and without jars,
> In wonted tones sang all the heavenly height.
> So when in death from underneath my feet
>   Rolls the round world, I then shall see the sky
>   Of God's truths burning yet familiarly;
> My native constellations I shall greet;
>   I lose the outer, not the inner eye,
>   The landscape, not the soul's stars, when I die.

God cannot give the wicked two chances without subjecting the good to two risks.

Self-evident truth shows that man is free.

Self-evident truth proves that man may attain a final permanence of character, good or bad, and in that state not lose freedom of will.

This may occur in the best possible universe, in which all things will of course work together for good to the good, and, therefore, of necessity, for evil to the evil.

In the heavens of the soul there ride unquenchable constellations, which assert that we alone are to blame if we do what conscience says we *ought* not to do. We are just as sure of the fact that we and only we are to blame when we do what conscience pronounces *wrong*, as we are of our own existence. Our demerit is a self-evident fact. All men take such guilt for granted. We know that we are responsible as surely as we all know that we have the power of choice. We know both facts from intuition. Our existence we know only by intuition, and by that same axiomatic evidence we know our freedom. How does sin originate in us? By a bad free choice. Just so it originated in the universe. But God brought us into existence. Yes; and he maintains us in existence. Very well; but the axioms of self-evident truth prove that he has given to us free will. The ocean floats the piratical vessels; the sea breeze fills the sails of the pirate; but neither the ocean nor the sea breeze is to blame for piracies.

VII. *Under irreversible natural law there can be no blessedness without holiness.*

Here I leave you, face to face with the nature of things, the authority which dazzled Socrates. God's omnipotence cannot force blessedness on a soul that has lost the predominant desire to be holy. Omniscience cannot make happy a man who loves what God hates and hates what God loves. If you fall into predominant dissimilarity of feeling with God, it is out of his power to give you blessedness. Undoubtedly we are, of all men, most miserable, unless with our deliverance from the guilt of sin there comes to us also deliverance from the love of it. Without holiness there can be no blessedness, but there can be no holiness without a predominant love of what God loves and hate of what God hates. We grow wrong; we allow ourselves to crystallize in habits that imply a loss of a desire to be holy; and, at last, having made up our minds not to love predominantly what God loves, and hate what he hates, we are amazed that we have not blessedness. But the universe is not amazed. The nature of things is but another name for the divine nature. God would not be God if there could be blessedness without holiness.

Mrs. Browning, whom England loves to call Shakespere's daughter, and who is, in many respects, the deepest interpreter of the modern cultivated heart and head, rests in God's goodness.

Oh, the little birds sang east; the little birds sang west!
And I said in underbreath: All our life is mixed with death,
And who knoweth which is best?

Oh, the little birds sang east; the little birds sang west!
And I smiled to think God's greatness flows around our incompleteness;
Round our restlessness his rest.

Had she paused there she would not have been the prophetess of science, as she is, for, without resting in an unscientific liberalism, she says also:

Let star-wheels and angel-wings, with their holy winnowings,
Keep beside you all your way,
Lest in passion you should dash, with a blind and heavy crash,
Up against the thick-bossed shield of God's judgment in the field.
                                      [Rime of the Duchess May.

# THE PROMINENCE OF THE ATONEMENT.

BY

PROF. EDWARDS A. PARK, D.D.

# THE PROMINENCE OF THE ATONEMENT.

### BY EDWARDS A. PARK, D.D.

---

*For I determined not to know anything among you, save Jesus Christ, and him crucified.* — 1 *Corinthians*, ii. 2.

SHOULD the apostle who penned this eloquent expression resume his ministry on earth, and should he deign to hold converse with us on the principles of his high calling, and should he repeat his strong words, — I am now, as of old, determined not to know anything among you save Jesus Christ, and him crucified, — some of us would feel an impulse to ask him:

"Can your words mean what they appear to imply? You are learned in Rabbinical literature; you have read the Grecian poets, and even quoted from Aratus; you have examined the statuary of Greece, and have made a permanent record of an inscription upon an altar in ancient Athens; you have reasoned on the principles of Aristotle from effect to cause, and have taken rank with the philosophers, as well as orators of the world; and now, you seem to utter your determination to abandon all knowledge save that which concerns the Jew who was crucified. You once said that you had rather speak five words with the understanding, than ten thousand words in an unknown tongue; and here, lest the pithy language of this text should fail of being truly apprehended, we desire to learn its precise meaning in three particulars:

"In the first place, do you intend to assert that our knowledge is controlled by our will? You *determined* not to know anything save one? Can you by mere choice expel all but one of your old ideas, and make your mind like a chart of white paper in reference to the vast majority of your familiar subjects of thought?"

'I am ready to concede,' is the reply, 'that much of our knowledge is involuntary; still a part of it is dependent on our will. In some degree, at some times, we may attend to a theme or not attend to it, as we choose, and thus our choice may influence our belief, and thus are we responsible, in a certain measure, for our knowledge. Besides, the word "know" is used by us Hebraistic writers to include not only a *mental* apprehension, but also a *moral* feeling. When we know Christ, we feel a hearty complacence in him. Again, to "know" often signifies to *manifest*, as well as to *possess*, both knowledge and love. We do not know an old acquaintance when we of set purpose withhold all public recognition of him, and act outwardly as if we were inwardly ignorant of his being. But I, Paul, say to you, as I said to the Corinthians, that I shall make the atonement of Christ, and nothing but the atonement of Christ, the main theme of my regard, of my loving regard, and such loving regard as is openly avowed.'

Thus our first query is answered; but there is a second inquiry which some of us would propose to the apostle, were he uttering to us personally the words which he wrote to the Corinthians. It is this:

"Should a Christian minister *out* of the pulpit, as well as *in* the pulpit, know nothing save the crucified one? Did *you* not know how to sustain yourself by the manufacture of tents; and did you not say to the circle of elders at Ephesus,—These hands have ministered to my necessities? Did you not dispute with the Roman sergeants—plead your cause before the Roman courts? Must not every minister cease for a time to converse on the work of Jesus; and must he not think of providing for his own household, lest he become worse than an infidel?"

'I am willing to admit,' is the reply, 'that the pulpit is the place where the minister should speak of Christ with more *uniform* distinctness than in other places; but there are no places, and no times, in which he should fail to manifest, more or less obviously, his interest in his Redeemer. Wherever he goes, he has a pulpit. Whether he eat, or drink, or whatever he do, he must do all for the glory of God, and the highest glory of God is Christ, and the highest honor of Christ is in him crucified. A minister must always respect the proprieties of life; in honoring them he *knows* that appropriate model man, who, rising from the tomb, wrapped up the napkin that was about his head, and laid it in a place by itself. Now the proprieties of life do require a minister to speak in the pulpit on themes more plainly and more easily connected with the atonement, than are various themes on which he must speak in the market-place or in the schools. But all subjects on which he may discourse do lead, sooner or later, more or less obviously and easily, to the great work of Jesus; and he should converse on them with the intent of seizing every hint they give him, following out every line to which they point him, in the direction of the cross. I have been in many synagogues, and in the temple, and on Mars' Hill, and on a Mediterranean ship-deck; and once was I hurried along in a night-ride from Jerusalem to Cæsarea with four hundred and seventy soldiers, horsemen and spearmen. I have resided at leisure with my arm chained to a Roman guard in a prison at the Capital of the Roman Empire; but in all such places I have felt, and everywhere I do feel, bound to speak out, and to act out, all the interest which the fitnesses of the occasion admit, in the atonement of Jesus; and not to manifest, and not to feel, any interest in any theme which may lessen my regard for this—the chiefest among ten thousand!'

But there is a third question which some of us would propose to the apostle, were he to speak in our hearing the words of the text:

"Should every *man*, as well as every minister, cherish and exhibit no interest in anything but Christ? Should a sailor at the mast-head, a surgeon in the extirpation of the clavicle, a warrior in the critical moment of the last charge, look at nothing, and hear of nothing, but the cross? Must not every one conduct businesses, and sustain cares, which draw his mind away from the atonement?"

'I am ready to grant,' is the reply, 'that some duties are less plainly and less intimately connected than others with the work of Jesus; but all of them are connected with it in some degree, and this connection may be seen by all who choose to gain the fitting insight. The great principle of duty belonging to the minister in the pulpit, belongs to him everywhere; and the great principle of duty belonging to the minister, belongs to every man, woman, and child. There is not one religion for the man when he is in the temple, and another religion for the man when he is in the parlor or in the street. There is not one law for the ordained pastor, and another law for the tradesman or the mechanic. The same law and no different one, the same religion and no different one, are the law and the religion for apostles, and publicans, and prophets, and taxgatherers, and patriarchs, and children, and nobles, and beggars. Every man is bidden to refuse everything, if it be the nearest friend, who interferes with the claims of the Messiah; and therefore every man, layman as well as clergyman, must keep his eye fixed primarily upon the cross. He may see other things within the range of that cross, but he must keep the cross directly at the angle of his vision, and allow nothing else, when placed side by side with the tree on Calvary, to allure his eye away from that central, engrossing object.'

Here, then, is our third question answered; and in these three replies to these three queries, we perceive the meaning of our text to be: that not on the first day only, but on every day likewise, not in the religious assembly only, but in all assemblies, and in all solitudes likewise, not the preacher only, but the hearer likewise,—every man must adopt the rule, to give his voluntary, his loving, his secret and open regard to nothing so much as to the character and work of his Redeemer.

Having inquired into the meaning of the apostle's words, let us proceed, in the next place, to inquire into the importance of making the atonement of Christ the only great object of our thought, speech, and action.

And here, did we hold a personal interview with the author of our text, we should be prompted to put three additional queries before him. Our first inquiry would be:

"Is not your theme too contracted? It is well to know Christ, but in all the varying scenes of life *is* it well not to know anything else. Will not the pulpit become wearisome if, spring and autumn, summer and winter, it confine itself to a single topic? We have known men preach themselves out by incessant repetitions of the scene at Calvary, — a scene thrilling in itself, and on that very account not bearing to be presented in its details, every Sabbath day. How much less will the varying sensibilities of the soul endure the reiteration of this tragic tale every day and at every interview! Such extreme familiarity induces irreverence. The Bible is not confined to this theme. It is rich in ecclesiastical history, political history, ethical rules, metaphysical discussion, comprehensive theology. It contains one book of ten chapters which has not a single allusion to God, and several books which do not mention Christ; why then do you shut us up to a doctrine which will circumscribe the mind of good men, and result in making their conversation insipid?"

'Contracted!' — this is the reply, — 'and do you consider this topic a limited one, whose height, depth, length, breadth, no finite mind can measure? Of what *would* you speak?'

"We would speak of the divine existence."

'But Christ is the "I am."'

"We would speak of the divine attributes."

'But Christ is the Alpha and Omega; *he* searcheth the reins and trieth the hearts of men; *he* is the same yesterday, to-day, and forever; full of grace and truth; to *him* belong wisdom and power and glory and honor; of *his* dominion is no end. Of what, then, *would* you speak?'

"We would speak of the divine sovereignty."

'But Christ taught us to say: Even so, Father, for so it seemed good in thy sight—and he and his Father are one.'

"We would converse on the divine decrees."

'But all things are planned for *his* praise who was *in* Christ, and *in whom* Christ was at the beginning.'

"We would discourse on electing love."

'But the saints are elect in Christ Jesus.'

"We would utter many words on the creation of men and angels."

'Now by our Redeemer were all things created that are in heaven and that are in the earth, visible and invisible."

"We would converse on the preservation of what has been created."

'Now Christ upholdeth all things by the word of his power. What *would* you have, then, for your theme?'

"We would take the flowers of the field for our theme."

'But they are the delight, as well as the contrivance of the Redeemer.'

"We would take for our theme the globes in space."

'But they are the work of his fingers.'

"Then we would take the very winds of heaven for our theme, lawless and erratic as they are."

'But Jesus taught us to comment upon these as an illustration of his truth. His poetic mind gave us the conception that the wind bloweth where it chooseth to blow; and we look on, wondering whence it cometh, and whither it goeth, knowing only that it is the breath of the Wonderful Counsellor, who arouseth it as he listeth, or saith, Peace, be still. What else, then, do you prefer for your topic of conversation?'

"We prefer the laws of nature for our topic."

'But in them the Father worketh and Christ worketh equally.'

"If it be so, we will select the fine and useful arts for our subject."

'But all the materials of these arts, and all the laws which compact them, and all the ingenuity which arranges them are of his architectonic plan. He is the guide of the sculptor, painter, musician, poet. He is the contriver of all the graces which we in our idolatry ascribe to the human discoverer, as if man had originally invented them. The history of the arts is the history of Christ's government on earth. Will you propose, then, some other theme for your remark?'

"Do let us converse on the moral law."

'You may; but Christ gave this law and came to magnify it.'

"Then let us comment on the ceremonial law."

'You may; but all its types are prophecies of Jesus.'

"Then we will expatiate on virtue in the general."

'Do so; but Christ is the first exemplar, the brightest representative of all abstract goodness, of all your virtue in the general.'

"Then we will take up ethical maxims."

'Take them up; but they are embodied in him who is the way, the truth, the life.'

"We will resort, then, to human responsibility for our subject of discourse."

'But we must all appear before the judgment seat of that fair-minded arbiter who is man as well as God.'

"May we not speak of eternal blessedness?"

'Yes; but it is Christ who welcomes his chosen into life.'

"Shall we not converse, then, on endless misery?"

'Yes; but it is Christ who will proclaim: Depart, ye cursed.'

"The human body;—we would utter some words on that."

'But your present body is the image of what your Lord wore once, and the body that you will have, if you die in the faith, is the image of what your Lord wears now;—the image of the body slain for our offenses and raised again for our justification.— And have you still a favorite theme which you have not suggested?'

"The pleasures of life are our favorite theme."

'Yes, and Jesus provided them and graced them at Cana.'

"The duties of the household are our favorite theme."

'Yes, and Jesus has prescribed them and disciplines you by them, and will judge you for your manner of regarding them.— What would you have, then, what can you think of for your choice topic of discourse?'

"We love to talk of our brethren in the faith."

'But they are indices of Christ, and he is represented by them.'

"We choose to converse on our Redeemer's indigent, imprisoned, diseased, agonized followers."

'And he is an hungered, athirst, penniless, afflicted in them, and whatsoever we do to one of them we do to him, and what we say of one of them we say of him.'

"May we speak in the pulpit of slaves?"

'Of slaves! Can you not speak of Medes and Parthians, Indians and Arabians? Why not then of Africans? Have they, or have they not, immortal souls? Was Jesus, or was he not, crucified for them? Was he ashamed of the lowly and the down-trodden, and those who have become the reproach of men and the despised of the people? You may speak of all for whom Christ died; as all men, bond or free, and all things, globes or atoms, suggest thoughts leading in a right line or in a curved line to the cross of Christ. All things, being thus nearly or remotely suggestive of the atonement, are for your sakes; whether Paul or Apollos, or Cephas, or the world, or life, or death, or things present, or things to come,— all are yours, for your thoughts, for your words. If things pertain to the divine essence, the whole of *that* is the essence of Jesus; if they pertain to the divine relations, all of *them* are the relations of Jesus; if they pertain to the noblest and brightest features of seraphs, all the angels of God bow down before Jesus; if they pertain to the minutest changes of human life, in all our vicissitudes Jesus keeps up his brotherhood with us; if they pertain to the vilest and darkest spot of our depravity, they pertain to Jesus,— for to speak aright of sin is to be determined to speak of Christ and of him crucified for sin.

'And is this the doctrine which men call a contracted one? Narrow! The very suspicion of its being narrow has now suggested the first reason why you should place it and keep it as the crown of all your words and deeds:— it is so large, so rich, so boundless, that you need nothing which excludes it. And therefore,' continues the Apostle, 'I mean to know and to love nothing, and to make it manifest that I care for nothing, in comparison with, and disconnected from, the God-man, as he develops all his attributes and all his relations on the cross.'

But were the author of these laconic words in a familiar conference with us, we might be tempted to address to him a second inquiry:

"Is not your theme too large? At first we deemed it too small, but now it swells out before us into such colossal dimensions that we change our ground, and ask: Can the narrow mind of man take in this multiplicity of relations, comprehended in both the natures, and in the redemptive, as well as all the other works of Christ? Do not our frail powers need one day as a day of rest, and one place as a sanctuary of repose, from every thought less tender than that of the atoning death itself? Must we not call in our minds from Christ *and* him crucified, so as to concentrate all our emotions on the simple fact of Christ crucified?"

'Too large a theme!'—this is the reply,—'it *is* a large theme, too large to be fully comprehended by finite intelligences. Men have dreamed of exhausting the atonement by defining it to be a plan for removing the obstacles which stand in the way of our pardon. It is too large for that definition, as the atonement also persuades the Most High to forgive us. Then men have thought to mark it round about by saying that it is a scheme for inducing God to interpose in our aid. But the atonement is too large for that defining clause, as it also presents motives to man for accepting the interposition of God. Then some have thought to define it *exactly*, by saying that the atonement is both an appeal to the Law-giver and also an appeal to the sinner. Too large still is the atonement for that explanation. It is an appeal to both God and man, but it is more. It is an appeal to the universe, and is as many-sided as the universe itself is to be variously affected. Can we by searching find out the whole of atoning love ? It is the love of him who stretched out his arms on the fatal wood, and pointed to the right hand and to the left hand, and raised his eyes upward, and cast them downward; and thus all things above and below, and on either side, he embraced in his comprehensive love. It *is* a large theme, but not too large to operate as a motive upon us. The immeasurable reach of a motive is the hiding of its power. The mind of man is itself expansive, and requires and will have something immense and infinite of truth or error, either overpowering it for good or overmastering it for evil. The atonement *is* a great theme, but not too great; and for this additional reason,— its greatness lies, in part, in its reducing all other doctrines to a unity, its arranging them around itself in an order which makes them all easily understood. We know in other things the power of unity amid variety.

We know how simple the geography of a land becomes by remembering that its rivers, although meandering in unnumbered circuits around the hills and through the vales, yet pursue one main direction from one mountain to one sea. Now all the truths of God flow into the atonement. *They are understood by means of it,* because their tendencies are toward it; and *it is understood by means of them,* because it receives and comprehends them.

'Consider more fully the first part of this sentence; *all other truths are understood by means of the atonement.* It gives to them all a unity by illustrating them all. Other truths are not so much independent themes, as they are branches growing up or side-wise out of this one root, and they need this single theme in order that their relations may be rightly understood. What, for example, *can* we know in its most important bearings, unless we know the history and office of our Redeemer? Begin from what point we may to examine the uses of things, we can never measure their full utility until we view them from the cross. The trees bud and blossom. Why? To bear fruit for the sustenance of the human body. But is this an ultimate object? The nourishment of the body favors the growth of the mind. But is the human mind an end worthy of all the contrivances in nature? Does the sun, with all its retinue of stars, pursue its daily course with no aim ulterior to man's welfare? Do we adopt a Ptolemaic theory in morals, that man is the centre of the system, and other worlds revolve around him? All things were made for God, as the Being in whom they all terminate. Do they exist for elucidating his power? This is not his chief attribute. His knowledge? There is a nobler perfection than omniscience. His love? But there is one virtue imbedded as a gem in his love, and his love is but a shining casket for this pearl of infinite price. This pearl is grace. This is the central ornament of the character of Jehovah. But there is no grace in Jehovah save as it beams forth in Christ; not in Christ as a mere Divinity, nor in Christ as a mere spotless humanity, but in the two united, and in that God-man crucified. All things were made *by* him and *for* him, rising from the cross to the throne. Without reference to him in his atoning love, has nothing been made that was made in this world. The star in the East led wise men *once* to the manger where the Redeemer lay; and all the stars of heaven lead wise men *now* to him who has risen above the stars, and whose glory illumines them all. He is termed the sun of righteousness; and, as the material sun binds all the planets around it in an intelligible order, so does Christ shine over, and under, and into, and through all other objects, attract them all to himself, marshal them all into one clear and grand array, showing them all to be his works, all suggestive of our duty, our sin, our need of atonement, our dependence on the one God, and the one Mediator between God and man.

'The first part of my sentence was, All other truths are understood by means of the atonement. Consider next the second part: *The atonement is understood by means of other truths.* It crystallizes them around itself, and reduces them into a system, not only because it explains them, but also because it makes them explain it. It is not too large a theme for all the sciences and the arts bring their contributions to make it orderly and plain. Our text is a simple one, because its words are interpreted by a thousand facts shining upon it, and making themselves and it luminous in their radiations around and over it. Listen again to its suggestive words:

"For I determined not to know any thing among you save Jesus Christ, and him crucified."

'Now, what is the meaning of this plain term, "*Christ?*" It means a "king." But how can we appreciate the king, unless we learn the nature of the beings over whom he rules? He reigns over the heavens; *therefore* we investigate the heavens. The whole earth is full of his glory; *therefore* we study the earth. He is the Lord over the angels; when we reflect on them, we catch a glimpse of him in his regal state. He is the King of the Jews and the Gentiles. When we meditate on men, we enjoy a glance at him who was born for this end, that he might have dominion over our race. When we contemplate the material worlds, all the vastness and the grandeur included in them, — the sphere of mind, all the refinement and energy involved in it, — we are overpowered by the reality, surpassing fable, that he who superintends all the movements of matter and first spake it into being, and once framed, as he now governs, the souls of his creatures, — he is the King who atoned for us; and the more we know of the stars in their courses, and of the spirit in its mysteries, so much the deeper is our awe in view of the condescending pity which moved their Creator to become one with a lowly creature acquainted with grief for you and me. So much is involved in the word, "Christ."

'But our text speaks of *Jesus* Christ. That word, "Jesus!" What is the meaning of it? It means a "deliverer," and in the view of some interpreters it means "God, the deliverer." Deliverer? From what? We do not understand the power of his great office, unless we learn the nature and the vileness of sin; and we have no conception how mean, how detestable, sin is, unless we know the needlessness of it, the nobleness of the will which degrades itself into it, the excellence of the law which is dishonored by it. All our studies, then, in regard to the nature of the will, the unforced voluntariness of depravity, the extent of it through our race, the depth of it, the purity of the commands aiming to prevent it, the attractions of virtue, the strangeness of their not prevailing over the temptations of vice, — they are not mere metaphysics; — they are studies concerning the truth and the grace of Immanuel, who is *God with us*, and whose name is "Deliverer" because he delivers his people from their sins; sins involving the power and the penalty of free wrong choice; a penalty including the everlasting punishment of the soul; a punishment suggesting the nature and the character of the divine law, and the divine Lawgiver, in their relation to the conscience and all the sensibilities of the mind; and that mind, as undying as its Maker. All these things are comprehended in the word, "Jesus."

'But our text speaks of Jesus Christ and *him crucified:* and this third term, "crucified," adds an emphasis to the two preceding terms, and stirs us up to examine our own capabilities, — to learn the skill pervading our physical organism, so exquisitely qualified for pain as well as pleasure; the wisdom apparent in our mental structure, so keenly sensitive to all that can annoy as well as gratify; and thus we catch a glimpse of the truth, that he who combines all of our dignity with none of our guilt, and with all of the divine glory, and who thus develops all that is fit to be explained in man, and all that can be explained in God, — he it is who chose to hang and linger with aching nerve and bleeding heart upon the cross for you and me. This cross makes out an atonement of the sciences and the arts, and brings *them* also, as well as devout men, at one with God; all of them tributary to the doctrine that we are bought with a price,—that we are redeemed, not with silver and gold, but with the precious blood of a man, who was God manifest in the flesh.—Too large a theme is the atonement? But it breaks down the middle wall of partition that has kept apart the different studies of men; and it brings them together as illustrations of the truth, which in their light becomes as simple as it is great.

'The very objection, then, that the redemptive work is too extensive for our familiar converse, has suggested the second reason why it should be the main thing for us to think upon, and speak upon, and act upon: It systematizes all other themes, and gains from them a unity which becomes the plainer because it is set off by a luminous variety; and for this cause,' continues the apostle, 'I intend to know nothing with supreme love, except this centralizing doctrine which combines all other truths into a constellation of glories.'

There is still a third inquiry which we might present to the author of our text, could we meet him in a personal colloquy:

"Your words all converge toward one point; will they not then become monotonous, and inapposite to the varying wants of various, or even the same individuals?

'A monotonous theme!'—this is the reply: 'What can be more diversified than the character and work of him who is at one time designated as the omniscient God, and at another time as a mechanic; at one time as a judge, and at another time as an intercessor; now a lion, and then a lamb; here a vine, a tree, there a way, a door; again a stone, a rock, still again a star, a sun; here without sin, and there he was made sin for us.

'Monotonous is this theme? Then it is sadly wronged, and the mind of man is sadly harmed; for this mind shoots out its tendrils to grasp all the branches of the tree of life, and the tree in its healthy growth has branches to which every sensibility of the human mind may cling. The judgment is addressed by the atonement, concerning the nature of law, of distributive justice, the mode of expressing this justice either by punishing the guilty or by inflicting pain as a substitute for punishment, the influence of this substitution on the transgressor, on the surety, on the created universe, on God himself. There is more of profound and even abstruse philosophy involved in the specific doctrine of the atonement, than in any other branch of knowledge; and there has been or will be more of discussion upon it, than upon all other branches of knowledge; for sacred science is the most fruitful of all sciences in logical deduction, and this specific part of the science is the richest of all its parts.

'Not only the judgment, but also the imagination is addressed by the atonement; as this is the comprehensive event pointing to those three several hours, the like to which have never been heard of, no, nor ever shall be: that first hour, the hour of humiliating change, when the Son of God, who had been from the beginning with God, gathering in the praises of angels and enjoying the honors of his universal reign, on a sudden left the bosom of his Father, and choirs of angels followed far off from his train, and heralded to the shepherds his arrival on earth;—and that second hour, the hour of gloom, when the only-begotten Son, smitten of the Father, cried out with a loud voice at the heaviness of the blow, and the earth was astonished more than when the prophet asked of old: Was the Lord displeased against the rivers? Was thine anger against the rivers? Was thy wrath against the sea?— and that third hour, the hour of triumph, when his troops of heralds shouted at his arrival: Lift up your heads, O ye gates; and be ye lift up, ye everlasting doors, and the King of glory shall come in, scarred in his hands and feet and side, but over all his foes victorious, and marching from his cross to his throne, —and let all the angels of God now worship him! What was the appearance of heaven, how did its hosts look during that first hour, when the very light of heaven moved out of its place, and descended gracefully like a star to Bethlehem. And what was the solemnity in heaven, what was the deed done there, during that second hour, when the first Person withdrew himself from the second Person, and the angels veiled their faces at the unutterable solitude of him who trod the wine-press alone? And what was the festival in the realm of joy during that third hour, when its monarch came riding prosperously home, with his sword upon his thigh, and all the hearts of the redeemed threw open their doors for his glad entrance — a conqueror, and more than conqueror, welcome, welcome to his everlasting rest! At these three scenes, in a life all full of transporting eras, the imagination falters, and lingers around them, and loses itself in a strange delight; and whether it be in the body or out of the body, it cannot tell. And will you say that scenes like these are monotonous?'

"Not so for the poet or the philosopher," we might reply, "but are they variously appropriate for the common mind?"

'The common mind!'— this is the rejoinder. 'The common mind is reached first of all by the Atonement. Those children who cried "hosanna" in the temple are yet in our eye as pictures of thousands of children, who feel and love the divine attributes as they are made plain and well-nigh tangible in Jesus. Simeon and Anna yet stand in that same temple as statues representing hundreds of aged saints, who love to read the history of their Redeemer when all other letters become illegible, and who can hear his voice when all other voices become inaudible, and who grow young again as his fresh doctrine rejuvenates their heart. Zaccheus climbing the sycamore still remains in our vision as a symbol of many a rich extortioner, who cannot rest until he has entertained his Lord, and consecrated the half of his goods to the poor, who are to be always with him, reminding him of their Redeemer. That widow weeping as she measures her slow steps out of the city, and smiling through her tears as she receives her son healthy from the bier on which he was borne toward the needlessly opened tomb, yet continues in our view as a representative of many a mourner relieved by his timely charities. Those minstrels who laughed him to scorn are images of millions who despise him; and then he blesses them, and then with glad voice they spread the fame of him round about; the fame of him whose mission it is to render good for evil, and to be the friend of his foes. If I desire to be soothed, I find nowhere such gentleness as at his last supper. If I aim to be stimulated, I find nothing like his crown of thorns stirring me to duty. If I need to be joyous, whither shall I go but to him, all whose garments smell of myrrh, and aloes, and cassia out of the ivory palaces, whereby they have made him glad?

'The very intimation that the Atonement addresses only one sensibility, and is appropriate to only one class of men, in one mood of mind, has now suggested the third reason why this doctrine should be the main spring of our inward and outward enterprise: It is so flexile and multiform, that it must be apposite to every man in every change of character or state; and therefore,' continues the apostle, 'I desire to make nothing prominent in my inward thought or outward life, except this ever-fitting truth of Jesus Christ and him crucified!'

Having now stated three reasons why it is important to make the redemptive scheme our main object of interest, let us close this discourse with three brief inquiries into the method of giving the desired prominence to this wonderful scheme.

And, first, were we conversing face to face with the author of our text, when he had become Paul the aged and the counsellor, we might ask him:

"In what method shall we resist our natural disinclination to make the grace of Christ so conspicuous? Is there not such a disinclination? Will not your hearers, will not you yourself, much more, shall not we who have never been caught up to the third heaven, feel tempted to elevate self above the redemptive mercy?"

'I fear it;'—this is the reply,—'I fear it for myself. Many secret misgivings have disturbed me. I know the need of watchfulness. But I have a fixed *resolve*. If any man be tempted to find some less humbling theme, I more; circumcised the eighth day, of the stock of Israel, of the tribe of Benjamin, an Hebrew of the Hebrews, as touching the law a Pharisee (after the most straitest sect I lived a Pharisee), as touching the righteousness of the law blameless. Yet *I am determined* to count all these things as loss, that I may win Christ.

'You inquire about my hearers. They *will* prefer to gratify their self-esteem, rather than receive the excellency of the knowledge of Jesus. I have tried them again and again. I knew the pride of Corinth when I avowed to her citizens: I am determined to know nothing among *you* save Jesus Christ, and him crucified. I knew then that Corinth was called, The Wealthy. For more than eighteen months I dwelt within her proud walls. I met her glad citizens on the Acrocorinthus, enjoying their magnificent scenery. I saw them going down the marble steps of their fountain Peirene, where their famed Pegasus, as they believed, was caught by Bellerophon. I visited their Stadium, and I drew one of my illustrations from it. I looked in upon their Theatre, and was moved by it to exclaim: We are become a Theatre to the world, to angels, to men. I beheld the gay throngs at the Corinthian Amphitheatre, that edifice so massive that the remains of it, as also of their Stadium and their

Theatre, are yet to be seen, and long after your dying day will be visited and admired by your own countrymen. It is true, I did feel often that those votaries of pleasure would look upon my preaching of the cross as foolishness in comparison with their rounds of festivity. But none of these things moved me. I was not ashamed of the Gospel of Christ. *I had a fixed plan.* I wrote from Corinth to the very capital of the world: So much as in me is, I am ready to preach the Gospel to you who are at Rome also. Wherever I went, I knew that bonds and imprisonment awaited me for my chief theme of discourse, yet I was *determined* to confer not with flesh and blood; for I said: A necessity is upon me; yea, woe is me if I preach not the Gospel of Christ even in the palaces of Corinth and of Rome. And if *my* steadfast resolution helped me to resist my own and my hearers' pride in the brilliant cities of the East, then *your* set resolve will nerve you anywhere, everywhere, to the same humbling service.

'Here, then, is the first method in which you may keep up the habit of making Jesus and him crucified, the soul of all your activity: Bring to your help the force of a resolute determination. There is a tendency in this resolute spirit to divert your thoughts from other themes, to turn the current of your sensibilities into the right channel, to invigorate your choice, to exert a direct and reflex influence in confirming the whole soul in Jesus. God is in that determination. He inspires it. He invigorates it. He works with it and by it. There is a power in it, but the power is not yours; it is the power of God. God is in every holy resolve of man.'

In our interview with the apostle we should address to him a second inquiry:

"In what method can we avoid both the fact and the appearance of being slavishly coerced into the habit of conversing on Christ and on Christ alone? You speak of taking your stand, adhering to your decision; but this dry, stiff resolve,—comes any genial spirit from it? Will you not be a slave to your unswerving purpose? Your inflexible rule,—will it not be a hard one, wearisome to yourself, disagreeable to others? You hold up a weighty theme by a dead lift."

'I *am* determined,'—this is the reply,—'and it is not only a strong, but it is a *loving* resolve. For the love of Christ constraineth me; whom having not seen in the flesh I love; in whom, though now I see him not, yet believing, I rejoice with joy unspeakable and full of glory. It is not a business-like resolution. It is not a diplomatic purpose. It is not a mechanical force. It is an affectionate decision. It is a joyous rule. It is the effluence of a supreme attachment to the Redeemer.

'And this is the second method in which you may retain Jesus Christ as the jewel of your speech and life: Cherish a loving purpose to do so. A man has strength to accomplish what with a full soul he longs to accomplish. Your Christian toil will be irksome to you, if it be not your cordial preference; but if your undeviating resolve spring out of a hearty choice of your Saviour, then will it be ever refreshed and enlivened by your outflowing, genial preference; then will your pious work be the repose of your soul. There is a power in your love to your work. It is a power to make your labor easy for yourself and attractive to others. This is not *your* power; it is the power of God. He enkindles the love within you. He enlivens it. He gives it warmth. He makes it instinct with energy. God is in all the holy joy of man.

In our conference with the author of our text we might suggest to him our third and last inquiry:

"In what method can we feel sure of persevering in this habitual exaltation of Christ? You speak of your stern purpose, but can you depend upon the continuance of it? You speak of your cordial as well as set resolve. But who are you? (forgive our pertinacious query.) Jesus we know. But his disciples, his chief apostles — is not every one of them a reed shaken with the wind, tossed hither and thither, unstable as a wave upon the sea?"

'I know it is so,'—this is the reply. 'Often am I afraid lest, having preached the Gospel to others, I should be a castaway. And after all I am persuaded that nothing,—height, depth, life, death, nothing shall be able to separate me from the love of Christ; for I put my confidence in him, and while my purpose is inflexible and affectionate, it is also inwrought with *trust* in the atonement and the intercession. I *do* pursue my Christian life in weakness and in fear and in much trembling. For all the piety of the best of men is in itself as grass, and the goodliness thereof as the flower of the field. Therefore serve I the Lord with all humility of mind and with many tears and temptations. Yet I am *determined* with a *confiding* love. I *am* troubled on every side; my flesh has no rest; without are fightings, within are fears; in presence I am base among you, my bodily presence is weak and my speech contemptible; and if I must needs glory, I will glory in the things which concern my infirmities. Still, after all, *I am determined*, my right hand being enfolded in the hand of my Redeemer. I know whom I have believed, and am persuaded that he is able to keep that which I have committed unto him against that day. For my conversation is in heaven, from whence I am to look for the Saviour, the Lord Jesus Christ, who shall change our vile body that it may be fashioned like unto his glorious body, according to the mighty working whereby he is able to subdue all things unto himself. I say the truth in Christ; I lie not; I am the least of the apostles, that am not meet to be called an apostle, because I injured the church of God; I am less than the least of all saints. Still I am determined; for by the grace of God I am what I am; and this grace which was bestowed upon me was not in vain, but I labored more abundantly than they all; yet not I but the grace of God which was with me; for I can do all things through Christ which strengtheneth me, and *therefore I am determined.*

'Borne onward, therefore, by your fixed plan, and no one can succeed in anything without a plan, yet you must never rely ultimately upon your determined spirit. Allured further and further onward by your delight in your plan, and no one can work as a master in anything without enthusiasm in his prescribed course, still you must not place your final dependence upon your affectionate spirit; for if you take, for your last prop, either the sternness or the cheerfulness of your own determination, then you will *know* your determination, and you are *not* to know *anything* save Jesus Christ and him crucified. Here, then, is the third method in which you may give the fitting prominence to the best of themes: You must rest for your chief and final support on him and only on him, from whom all wise plans start, by whom they all hold out, to whom they all tend, who is all and in all, Jesus Christ and him crucified.'

My Christian brethren, you are all apostles. Every man, every woman, every child, the richest and the poorest, the most learned and the most ignorant of you — who have come up hither to dedicate yourselves and this sanctuary\* to your Lord, all being *sent* of him to serve him, have in fact and in essence the same responsibility resting on you as weighed on the author of our text. And he was burdened by the same kind of temptations and fears which oppress your spirit. But he was held up from failing in his work by a three-fold cord; and that was his resolute determination, as loving as it was resolute, and as trustful as it was loving, to know nothing save Jesus Christ and him crucified. The last that you hear of him as an *impenitent* man is in the words: "And Saul, yet breathing out threatening and slaughter against the disciples of the Lord." It was Christ whom the proud Jew last opposed. The first that you hear of him as a *convicted* man is in the words: "Who art thou, Lord?" It was Christ whom the inquiring Jew first studied. And the first that you hear of him as a *penitent* man is: "Lord, what wilt thou have me to do?" It was Christ to whom the humble disciple first surrendered his will. And the first that you hear of him as a Christian *minister* is: "And straightway he preached Christ in the synagogues that he is the Son of God." And the last

---

\* This sermon was preached at the dedication of the Broadway Tabernacle, New York, April 24, 1859.

that you hear of him as a Christian *hero* is: "I have fought the good fight, I have finished my course. I have kept the faith; henceforth there is laid up for me a crown of righteousness." And the secret of this victorious career is in words like those of our text: 'I adhered to my plan (when among the fickle Corinthians), I was decided (when among the vacillating Galatians), to know nothing (when among the learned at Athens and them of Cæsar's household at Rome); save Jesus Christ (when I was among my own kinsmen, who scorned him), and him crucified (when I was among the pupils of Gamaliel, all of whom despised my chosen theme); still I was determined to cling to that theme among the Greeks and the barbarians, before Onesimus the slave and Philemon the proud master; for I loved my theme, and, suffering according to the will of God, I committed the keeping of my soul to him in well-doing as unto a faithful Creator.'

And herein is it to be your plan, my brethren, and your joy, not to make this sanctuary the resort of wealth and of fashion, but rather of humble suppliants, who by their prayers may divert all the wealth and fashion of the world into the service of your Lord; not to make this temple the resting-place of hearers who shall idly listen to the words of an orator, but a temple of earnest co-workers with Christ,—thinking of him, speaking of him, loving him first, and last, and midst, and without end. As you come to this house of

God on the Sabbath, as you go from it, as your weekday recollections gather around it, may you renew and confirm your plan to know your Redeemer, and not only to know him, but — who is sufficient for these things ? — not to know any thing save your Redeemer; and not only to shut yourselves up to the supreme love of nothing except Christ, but also, — his grace will be sufficient for you, — to worship and serve Christ in the central relation of him crucified. Knowing him alone, he will sustain you as fully as if he knew you alone. He will come to you in this temple as frequently as if he had no other servants to befriend. He will listen to your prayers as intently as if no supplications came up to him from other altars, and he will intercede for you as entirely as if he interceded in behalf of no one else; for remember, that when he hung upon the cross, he thought of you, and died for you, just as fully as if he had been determined to think of no one, and to die for no one, save you, whom he now calls to the solemn service of consecrating your own souls, and your "holy and beautiful house" to the glory of Jesus Christ and him crucified.

www.ingramcontent.com/pod-product-compliance
Lightning Source LLC
Chambersburg PA
CBHW030010240426
43672CB00007B/890